The Language of Religion

HORIZONS IN PHILOSOPHY

GENERAL EDITORS:

JUDE DOUGHERTY

THE CATHOLIC UNIVERSITY OF AMERICA
WASHINGTON, D. C.

ROBERT WOOD

ST. JOSEPH'S COLLEGE, COLLEGEVILLE, INDIANA

The Language of Religion is one of the volumes in the *Philosophy and God* section of the series.

The Language of Religion

James I. Campbell
Eisenhower College
Seneca Falls, New York

The Bruce Publishing Company / New York
Collier-Macmillan Limited / London

The author and publisher of *The Language of Religion* are grateful to the following for permission to reprint copyrighted materials:

Random House, New York, for excerpts from "St. Anselm, Proslogion" in *The Wisdom of Catholicism,* by Anton C. Pegis, published in 1949.

The Macmillan Company, New York, for excerpts reprinted with permission of The Macmillan Company from *New Essays in Philosophical Theology,* edited by Anthony Flew and Alasdair MacIntyre, first published in 1955.

Harper & Row, Publishers, New York, for summary based on pages 72–77 and 160–165 of *Language, Logic and God,* by Frederick Ferre.

Library of Congress Catalog Card Number: 76-121005

THE BRUCE PUBLISHING COMPANY, NEW YORK
COLLIER-MACMILLAN CANADA, LTD., TORONTO, ONTARIO

Made in the United States of America

Acknowledgments

I am grateful to many persons who have helped me in the writing of this book. Dr. James S. Churchill and Dr. John Vollrath of Purdue University at Fort Wayne, and Dr. Robert S. Turley of the University of Notre Dame were kind enough to read portions of the manuscript and contributed many valuable insights and suggestions. The library staff of Indiana-Purdue Universities at Fort Wayne, and especially Miss Louise Sample, were unfailingly cooperative, efficient, and courteous. Mrs. Sondra Roth Mochson of The Bruce Publishing Company rendered invaluable editorial advice and assistance, and Prof. Warren Blackstone of Eisenhower College helped in proofreading the manuscript. I am permanently indebted to Dr. Harry Nielsen of the University of Windsor, teacher without peer, who introduced me to this area of philosophy. I wish to thank the general editors, Dr. Jude Dougherty and Dr. Robert Wood, for their invitation to contribute to this series. And my wife's encouragement, understanding, patience, and friendship made it all worthwhile. To her, and to my parents, this book is dedicated.

Contents

At present we are men looking at puzzling reflections in a mirror. The time will come when we shall see reality whole and face to face!

St. Paul, The First Letter to the Christians at Corinth, 13:12.

I

The Philosophy of Religion

What is the philosophy of religion? What are its concerns? To what branch of philosophy does it belong? In what way is it related to questions about the relationship between philosophy and religion or theology, reason and revelation?

Since its beginning, Western philosophy has been closely tied to religious belief and theological speculation. The relationship has not always been peaceful or amicable. If some thinkers have taught a perfect harmony between reason's discoveries and revealed truth, others have insisted that there is a bitter hostility between the two. The later philosophers of ancient Greece found little to admire in Olympian religion and turned their backs upon it, either, as Democritus did, to advocate that man's life ought to be conducted without reference to the divine or to the expectation of an afterlife, or to sneer at the anthropomorphic deities of Olympus and, as Xenophanes did, to speak instead of a God who was one, supreme among gods and men, and wholly unlike ordinary mortals.[1] The tales of the gods the poets told were held to be patently ridiculous if taken at face value, although some, like Aristotle, found value in them if they were interpreted as containing important natural truths.[2] By the end of the period of ancient philosophy, most educated men sought guidance, inspiration, and truth for their lives not from popular religions but from neo-Platonism, Stoicism, Epicureanism, and the other philosophical schools that presided over the end of an era.

---

[1] T. V. Smith, ed., *Philosophers Speak for Themselves*, 4 vols. (Chicago: University of Chicago Press, 1956–1957), 1:14.

[2] Aristotle, *Metaphysics*, XII, 8, 1074^{b}1–14, in *The Basic Works of Aristotle*, ed. Richard McKeon (New York: Random House, 1941). All subsequent references are to this edition.

The medieval period marked a gradual development of the belief that in principle, no conflict could occur between reason and revelation, provided each was scrupulously kept within its proper sphere of operation. As the view was argued by St. Thomas Aquinas, they could even lend fruitful assistance to one another in their separate endeavors. On behalf of revelation, reason could seek to provide rational demonstration of those truths, such as the existence of an all-perfect God, that are necessary for theology's "scientific" status; it could help dissipate objections which might keep an individual from faith; and it could aid men in understanding that which they held by faith by explicating the content of revelation and showing its developing relevance to their lives. Reason had on her own but weakly grasped some truths that were within her province, such as the human soul's immortality, but since God had revealed them anyway (since they are necessary for salvation), such revelation could not fail to benefit reason by encouraging her to seek rational proof of them with greater confidence in her own abilities. Then, too, since reason had been darkened by sin and was prone to error, revealed truth could at times guide her on her search for truth by pointing to errors into which she might have otherwise fallen.[3]

But this was by no means a unanimous view of the matter. There were those theologians in Aquinas' own time who sought to keep reason and rational methods wholly apart from revelation in order to maintain the purity of faith. There were also members of the Averroist tradition who taught a double standard of truth, one for faith and the other for reason, such that a truth of faith could be contradicted by a truth of reason, yet both could still be held as true.

Modern and contemporary philosophers handled these questions in ways that would have bewildered the medieval mind. The First

---

[3] St. Thomas Aquinas, *Summa Theologiae,* I, 1, 1–8; *Summa Contra Gentiles,* I, 3–8, and II, 2–4; in *D. Thomae Aquinatis Opera Omnia,* ed. S. Frette and P. Mare, 32 vols. (Paris: L. Vives, 1871–1880). Quotations from the *Summa Theologiae* are from its translation by the Fathers of the English Dominican Province, 3 vols. (New York: Benziger, 1947).

Mover that reason had demonstrated Aquinas identified with the God of Christianity. But this identification, not to say the demonstration itself, began to give way; by the sixteenth century Pascal cried for the God of Abraham, Isaac, and Jacob rather than the God of the philosophers. While the God whom medieval man adored called on man to account for his actions, Leibniz turned the tables when, at grips with the problem of evil, he felt constrained to justify God's ways to man. Hume severely limited man's ability to know whatever God or gods there are and dismissed revealed religion as superstition, useful anyway because its promise of an afterlife of rewards and punishments helps insure a law-abiding and peaceful citizenry. God was placed in the region of noumenal objects by Kant, unattainable by speculative reason but postulated by practical reason on behalf of morality. And in Hegel's interpretation, philosophy was superior to religion and theology, since these trafficked in *Vorstellungen* (rational truths clothed in images) whose rational form was the philosopher's concern.

In the hands of many nineteenth century European thinkers, religion came in for some penetrating and hostile criticism. There was the strong tendency to interpret and evaluate religion solely by reference to the social, economic, political, and psychological effects it had on man and society. The general consensus seems to have been that man could—and should—rid himself of religion. A call was issued for a new humanism that would take its point of departure in the renunciation of a God who was the archenemy of mankind; Kierkegaard's advocacy of a return to authentic Christianity, however, was a notable exception to this general trend. Auguste Comte taught that the human mind went through a religious, then a metaphysical, and finally a positivist, or scientific, state, with the religious state the most primitive, and with religious and metaphysical teachings inevitably giving way before the advance of science. Revelation was dead, and reason, worshipping humanity as its god, was to reign forever.

In the middle third of the nineteenth century, English philosophers abandoned a then-impoverished empiricism and turned for inspiration to Hegelian philosophy. But in the early years of this century, and for reasons that we shall sketch in the following chapter, the pendulum swung back, and English philosophy once again joined the empirical tradition. But the return involved a shift of emphasis. Philosophers, or those of them who came to be known as analysts,[4] took the proper business of philosophy to lie not in the study of reality or some portion of it, nor even precisely in the study of ideas or mental phenomena, but in the study of language. Consequently, the majority of interests that had become the hallmark of the philosopher's concern with religion were largely abandoned. No new God nobler than the God of popular religion was proposed, nor was there much professional interest in the social and personal advantages and disadvantages of religious belief. Such matters were proper to the cultural historian and to the special sciences like psychology and sociology. Indeed, the more radical of the earlier analysts declared that the issue of God's existence could not be discussed at all, since both "There is a God" and "There is no God" were statements lacking in cognitive content. Reason and revelation, philosophy and theology were not only *not* harmonious and complimentary, but revelation and theology, under attack by reason and philosophical methodology, were unworthy of the reflective man's serious consideration.

But times have changed; earlier "hard" positions have been softened and, in many cases, abandoned. The conception of a single kind of truth and meaning, that found in the positive sciences, has given way to more flexible and viable conceptions, so that it is now possible to suggest that religion might indeed deal in truth. The question of the existence of God once more commands the attention of some of the best analytic minds, and philosophical

---

[4] Analytic philosophers fall into one of two broad groupings: those who take the task of philosophy to be the analysis of *artificial* languages, constructed to be clearer and more precise than ordinary language (logical positivists); and those who take the task of philosophy to be the analysis of *ordinary* language (linguistic analysts). Although this distinction is not adequate in every case, we will use it as a general frame of reference. The term "analyst" as used in this work refers to both groups. See *Classics in Analytic Philosophy*, ed. Robert R. Ammerman (New York: McGraw-Hill Book Co., 1965), pp. 2–3 (hereafter cited as Ammerman, *Classics*).

analysis has come to be used, even by some theologians, as a valuable tool that can help one understand the language of religious belief and its relationship to other patterns of discourse.[5] Philosophers and theologians are starting again, with caution and hesitation, to discuss problems of mutual interest in a far less hostile atmosphere. They seem to be rediscovering that reason and revelation have much to gain from and give to one another. Philosophers are beginning to listen to what theologians say instead of telling them that they have nothing to say; theologians are finding that new philosophical methods and insights might help them in their endeavors.

Although the atmosphere has changed (and this has been no small accomplishment), the analysis of religious language is still the main interest of analytic philosophers of religion. This is not a philosophical novelty by any means. As early as the third century A.D. Dionysius, or Denis the Areopagite, wondered how ordinary language could be made to apply to a God who transcends all experience and all categories of human thought. Following him, Christian thinkers formulated and refined both the problem and the possible solutions to it. But natural theologians have always been primarily interested in the construction of purely rational proofs for God's existence and in coming to understand something of his attributes, while the problem of the meaningfulness of God-talk has taken a secondary, albeit important, position. For analysts the order of interest has changed, and primary attention is given to the nature and functions of religious discourse.

What, then, is the subject matter of the philosophy of religion? It would, no doubt, be widely taken to include all those philosophical issues implied or generated by religion (or theology) that we have indicated, although some of these might be listed under other headings as well—proofs for the existence of God under natural

[5] See, for example, the following works of Paul van Buren: *The Secular Meaning of the Gospel* (New York: The Macmillan Co., 1963); "Theology in the Context of Culture," *The Christian Century,* LXXXII, no. 14, April 7, 1965, pp. 428–430; "Christian Education *Post Mortem Dei,*" *Religious Education,* LX (1965), pp. 4–10; and "The Dissolution of the Absolute," *Religion in Life,* XXXIV (1965), pp. 334–342.

theology, for example. But some would include more than this. Professor Pringle-Pattison's *Studies in the Philosophy of Religion* written in the early 1930s includes essays on primitive religions, on the quest for the historic Jesus, on the Christ of the Creeds, and in the Christology of St. Paul. "It is the office of the philosophy of religion," he writes, "applying the insight gained in its historical and comparative review, to single out the characteristic and essential contribution of each religion in turn to the progress of mankind." [6] Most philosophers today, and certainly members of the analytic movement, would not consider such questions to be proper to philosophy at all, and would probably find fault with any attempt to chart the progress of religion in the terms suggested.

Although it might be impossible to draw exact boundaries around the philosophy of religion which would meet with general philosophical approval, it is somewhat easier to do so for analytically-oriented philosophy of religion. As there is general agreement that questions of language and meaning fall to the philosopher (and some would say it is his only subject-matter), the philosophy of religion could then be defined as that part of philosophy which investigates the language of religion or theology. While this would bear primarily on religious sentences themselves —their goals, epistemological foundations, the rules governing their usage, their relationship to statements in other areas of discourse, for example—it would also include the study of certain key terms and concepts operative in religious belief, such as *God, creation, miracle, immortal soul,* and the like. The philosophy of religion so defined is a part of epistemology. It is speculative in character and seeks to understand the nature of religious knowledge.

The philosophy of religion is related to religion in much the same way as the philosophy of science is related to science. This discipline takes as its subject matter the special sciences, and analyzes their language, concepts, terms, and categories. While this

---

[6] A. Seth Pringle-Pattison, *Studies in the Philosophy of Religion* (Oxford: Clarendon Press, 1930), pp. 9–10.

process may help the scientist to come to a deeper understanding of the foundations on which his work rests, thus affording some small benefit to the scientific enterprise, it is an incidental result of the philosopher's explorations. Similarly, while the philosopher's study of religious concepts, terms, and categories may provide a deeper understanding of the "logic" of belief to the theologian or to believers in general, this, too, is an incidental result.

This book is an introduction to the philosophy of religion as practiced by analytic philosophers. A restrictive note is necessary here. While some of the topics which we shall consider may bear on religion in general, it is Christianity with which English-speaking analysts are usually specifically concerned, and our examinations shall be similarly limited. Our focus will be, then, the main ways in which the statements of Christian religious belief are interpreted by members of this movement, although we shall consider a few nonanalytic views and the reactions of analysts to them. It would be far beyond the limits of this study to survey all the subsidiary questions connected with this central one. However, we shall examine an important one of these—the question of proofs for the existence of God—because it is of primary significance to the epistemological foundations of religious belief, and because it raises important problems whose dimensions have caused some to start to rethink older dogmatic stances, especially the one about the possibility of metaphysics.

Finally, this work does not aim at settling any of the issues investigated; many of them are so complex and so interwoven with others that all that can be reasonably hoped for is their clarification. Where some suggestions that might bear on solutions are made, this is done tentatively and with the realization that much more research and reflection are still necessary. If, however, this work contributes in some way to the understanding of these topics, it shall have accomplished its purpose.

II

Language and Contemporary English Philosophy

Well, but surely . . . you do not suppose that you can learn, or I explain, any subject of importance all in a moment; at any rate, not such a subject as language, which is, perhaps, the very greatest of all.

Plato, *Cratylus*, 427.

If we take in our hand any volume; of divinity or school meta-physics, for instance; let us ask, Does it contain any abstract reasoning concerning quantity or number? *No.* Does it contain any experimental reasoning concerning matter of fact and existence? *No. Commit it then to the flames: for it can contain nothing but sophistry and illusion.*

David Hume, *Enquiry Concerning Human Understanding*, III, 3.

Introduction

In this chapter we shall examine the change of direction that has occurred in recent English philosophy. We shall then investigate the views of language that have been influential among the majority of analytic philosophers, and shall note some of the consequences these views have for the language of religion.

The Rise of Analytic Philosophy

It has been widely held, and as widely denied, that English philosophy has undergone a profound and radical revolution in this century that marks it as a kind of mutant in the overall history of philosophy. Analytic thinkers, so the charge goes, refuse to seek and illuminate what may be called a "metaphysical dimension" of reality which is inaccessible to the positive sciences. Instead, they

8

take the analysis of language as the exclusive area of their concern. The result is that while a great deal of what they say might be important and even profound, most of it is unrelated to those great issues that are the province of philosophy as this discipline has been traditionally understood. Analysts hold that philosophical problems arise from a failure to understand the workings of language; some of them even maintain that a large portion of what has been commonly accepted as philosophy may be disregarded as meaningless chatter. To make matters worse, what is thus ignored turns out to be the very heart of the philosophical enterprise; in their hands philosophy has become impoverished and remote from the concerns of daily life. In sum, as one writer expressed it, analysts are not only fiddling while Rome burns; they are dismantling the fiddle.

Within the last 60 years there has been, without doubt, a marked change in the course of philosophy in England and English-speaking countries. But—avoiding the semantic hassle of "revolution" versus "evolution"—it can be reasonably argued that, paradoxically, this change both breaks and does not break with previous, and honorable, ways of doing philosophy. From earliest times, problems in the area of language and meaning have interested wise men. Plato's *Cratylus* and *Sophist* deal heavily in such questions; Aristotle methodologically begins many discussions from the ordinary and accepted meanings of terms and mounts linguistic attacks against his philosophical opponents (like Parmenides) that would do the most astute contemporary analyst proud.[1] In Book V of his *Metaphysics,* he treats elaborately of the meaning of some terms that are fundamental in the philosopher's lexicon. The medieval controversy over the universals is, in great part, an extended debate on how words mean. St. Thomas Aquinas (in question 13 of the *prima pars* of his *Summa Theologiae,* for example) expressed the medieval sage's interest in language and its relationship to the theological enterprise. William of Ockham and John Buridan, in the high middle ages, pursued research in

---

[1] See, for example, *Physics,* I, 7, 189^{b}30 ff. and his criticism of the Platonic Ideas in *Nicomachean Ethics,* I, 6.

philosophical linguistics, and not long after, Francis Bacon spoke of the linguistic snares that stand as one of the idols of a mind engaged in advancing the frontiers of knowledge. Locke, Berkeley, and Hume paid attention to words and how they conveyed meanings; and while 19th century continental philosophers were primarily engaged in building vast, all-encompassing systems to describe reality, they could still find time to consider language and its ability to depict what Reality was all about. The contemporary interest in language is not a philosophical novelty, nor is it without significant precedent in the history of western speculation.

But if there is continuity between the work of today's philosophers and those of the past, it is a *selective* continuity. Today's principal interests were secondary for many thinkers of the past whose dominant concerns have been cast off by contemporary English philosophers as not falling within the limits of their proper tasks. If one looks to philosophy to provide an account of reality other than that which can be gleaned from the sciences, or to give moral direction to human life, one would look in vain among the writings of most of the members of the analytic movement. Francis Herbert Bradley might have spoken of the Absolute's noninvolvement in the vicissitudes of daily life, but A. J. Ayer, upon investigation of Bradley's statement, will declare it lacking in meaning since there are no conceivable sense observations which would help one decide whether it is true or false. Philosophers of other traditions might discuss the rightness or wrongness of euthanasia; the analytic moralist probes into the logical status of ethical judgments and their relationship to other statements that function in other areas of discourse.

What caused this change, or rather, this tailoring of interest, in English philosophy? There were many causes, and it would take us too far afield to go into them all, or even into any one of them in detail. However, it might be valuable to trace some of the major ones in broad outline.

(1) *The wane of English neo-idealism.* About the middle of the nineteenth century, English thinkers began turning from a then dull and uninspired empiricism towards Hegelian metaphysics, es-

pecially as presented in the writings of J. F. Ferrier and John Grote. J. F. Stirling's *The Secret of Hegel* (1865) and Edward Caird's *Hegel* (1883), together with the publication of Jowett's translation of Plato's *Dialogues* (1871), hastened the move of English philosophy to the neo-Hegelian idealism that was to dominate it for the next half century.

The metaphysics of this philosophy was most prominently represented by F. H. Bradley. The world of common sense and science, he argued in his many works, especially in *Appearance and Reality* (1893), was not the *real* world at all, but only *appearance*. There were serious defects in the scientific worldview that could be finally resolved only if one adopted the metaphysical viewpoint. In place of a reality composed of separate, unique entities, metaphysics depicted reality as one—complete, systematic, and harmonious. This insight was attained in a vision that went beyond language and thought. Consequently, it could never be expressed in any finally satisfactory way, since language, the servant of conceptual thinking, always falsified it to some extent. The scientist was henceforth relegated to the exploration of the world of appearance, while the metaphysician saw Reality, and saw it whole and clear.

Born in the nineteenth century, Bradley's metaphysics was out of harmony with the spirit and inspiration of the twentieth. Whether or not science spoke of appearance rather than reality, there was little arguing with the fact that it was making extraordinary advances, its theoretical explorations matched by the practical ramifications these had in daily life. Many of the outstanding thinkers of the period were scientists or were sympathetic to the aims and goals of science. The philosophy that relegated science to the examination of that which was not the ultimately real could hardly be expected to command their loyalty. That philosophers did not unanimously accept Bradley's claim to be presenting the one ultimately satisfying view of reality, and that debate on issues as old as Parmenides still continued, led to further disenchantment with neo-idealist metaphysics.[2]

---

[2] For further discussion of the change in the interests of English philosophers, see the comprehensive study by John Passmore, *A Hundred Years of Philos-*

(2) *Bertrand Russell and G. E. Moore*. Both Russell and Moore led the attack on some of the fundamental theses of neo-idealism, in works that were marked by insight, technical brilliance, and close and subtle reasoning. In 1900 Russell began the attack on Bradley's denial of external relationships. Primarily concerned with science and mathematics, Russell believed that a theory of internal relations was essential if sense were to be made of basic categories of science and mathematics. Later on, he hit upon the insight that there was a disparity between the logical and grammatical form of some propositions. From this he developed the now classical theory of descriptions, which allowed him to give an adequate account of certain propositions that had engendered a great deal of philosophical and logical perplexity. It was Russell's influential view that an important philosophical task was the translation of grammatically misleading propositions into correct logical form.[3]

While Moore joined Russell in attacking Bradley's view of relations, he is best remembered for his vigorous defense of common-sense beliefs. In "The Refutation of Idealism" (1903) he attacked the proposition *esse est percepi* (to be is to be perceived), which, he maintained, is essential to all forms of idealism, but which he held to be false on the grounds that idealists had failed to distinguish the *awareness* of a sensation from the object of awareness, the sensation itself. In "A Defence of Common Sense" (1925) he argued that those who denied common-sense truths, or declared that they were at least partially false, were in error because they had failed to distinguish between the *truth* of these statements

ophy (New York: Basic Books, 1957), and G. J. Warnock, *English Philosophy Since 1900* (New York: Oxford University Press, 1966).

[3] Bertrand Russell, "What There Is," Chapter 8 of *Logic and Knowledge*, ed. R. C. Marsh (London: George Allen and Unwin, Ltd., 1956), reprinted in Ammerman, *Classics* (hereafter cited as Russell, "What There Is"). Cf. p. 26: "I think that practically all traditional metaphysics is filled with mistakes due to bad grammar, and that almost all the traditional problems of metaphysics and traditional results—supposed results—of metaphysics are due to a failure to make the kind of distinctions in what we may call philosophical grammar. . . ." An important application of Russell's belief about the interrelationship between philosophy and grammar can be found in his theory of descriptions, in Ammerman, *Classics*, pp. 15 ff.

and their *analysis*. The former was indubitable, the latter highly problematic.[4]

Both Russell and Moore advocated analysis as a proper philosophical technique. Geared to his interests in logic and science, Russell understood analysis as a means of resolving incomplete symbols and as a method for dispensing with abstractions.[5] By its use, he felt it would be possible to get down, at least in theory, to the "ultimate simples" (sense data), the ultimate metaphysical constituents of matter out of which all else is built.[6] Concerned with the epistemological bases of common-sense truths, Moore spoke of analysis as the technique whereby the relationship between sense data (or "sensa"), the immediate objects of perception, and things known by means of them is revealed.[7] A new era in philosophizing had now begun, with Russell and Moore providing not only new interests but the beginning of a new method as well.

(3) *The rise of logical positivism and Wittgenstein's* Tractatus. In 1919 Ludwig Wittgenstein published his doctoral dissertation, the *Tractatus Logico-Philosophicus*. This difficult work explored, among other topics, the nature of language and its relationship to facts. According to Wittgenstein, propositions are of two kinds: elementary (atomic) and complex (molecular). A complex statement is made up of more than one elementary statement (which, in turn, is made up of unanalyzable names), united by various logical connectives, such as "and," "if-then," "either-or," and the like. Complex propositions are truth-functional of elementary propositions, that is, they are true if their component elementary propositions are true.[8]

---

[4] G. E. Moore, "A Defence of Common Sense," reprinted in Ammerman, *Classics*, pp. 62–63, 66–67 (hereafter cited as Moore, "Defence").

[5] See Bertrand Russell, "Descriptions," Chapter 16 of *Introduction to Mathematical Philosophy* (London: George Allen and Unwin, Ltd., 1919), reprinted in Ammerman, *Classics*, pp. 15 ff.

[6] Russell, "What There Is," in Ammerman, *Classics*, pp. 26, 27, 29.

[7] Moore, "Defence," in Ammerman, *Classics*, pp. 64, 67.

[8] Ludwig Wittgenstein, *Tractatus Logico-Philosophicus*, trans. D. F. Pears and B. F. McGuiness (London: Routledge and Kegan Paul, 1961), props. 5 ff. This work is made up of a series of numbered propositions to which the cited numbers refer.

How is it possible for elementary propositions to mean something, to refer to something beyond themselves (facts)? This, Wittgenstein argued, is possible *only if* elementary propositions picture facts.[9] A proposition that does not picture a fact does not say anything at all; it has no *sense* whatever. Now since it is possible for the logical form of a proposition to be hidden by its grammatical form, Wittgenstein saw the task of philosophical analysis as the resolution of all complex propositions into their ultimate component parts, thereby revealing the isomorphic relationship between language and facts.

It was Wittgenstein's view that philosophical problems arose from the failure to realize the limits of language—failure, that is, to realize what could and could not be said. It was philosophy's task to make those limits clear. But if a proposition that did not picture a fact was without sense, it followed that philosophy was ultimately senseless, since it spoke not of facts but of the *relationship* between language and facts. Wittgenstein came to see his *Tractatus* as a compilation of statements which, to use his own metaphor, could be used as a ladder on which one climbed in order to command a clear view of things. Once this view had been attained, the ladder had to be kicked away.[10] The *Tractatus* ended on the bleak, and much-quoted, note: "What we cannot speak about we must pass over in silence." [11]

Although they disagreed with this final conclusion of the *Tractatus,* the members of the Vienna Circle of Logical Positivism greeted the work with enthusiasm and admiration. The Circle had been formed shortly after the publication of Moritz Schlick's *Space and Time in Contemporary Physics* (1917) and dissipated at the outbreak of World War II. Its members were Europe's leading scientists, mathematicians, and philosophers, among them Herbert Feigl, Victor Kraft, Rudolf Carnap, Frederick Waismann, and Kurt Goedel. Other leading thinkers, like Einstein, Planck,

---

[9] *Ibid.*, 2.1–2.1511; 2.182–2.201; and 2.202–3.02.
[10] *Ibid.*, 6.54.
[11] *Ibid.*, 7.

Hilbert, and Russell, were cognizant of the Circle's developing views through contacts with its members.[12]

In 1936 A. J. Ayer's *Language, Truth and Logic* was published, an articulate, highly-readable work that brought leading positivist ideas to the general attention of English-speaking philosophers. The radical approach which positivism espoused was apparent from the title of the book's first chapter, "The Elimination of Metaphysics." The death of metaphysics had been proclaimed before, of course, most notably by David Hume and Immanuel Kant. What was unique to the positivist condemnation was the idea that metaphysics was impossible because its assertions could not possibly be empirically verified. As such verification, for reasons we shall examine later, was declared to be a condition *sine qua non* for meaningful language, the utterances of the metaphysician were declared to be simply without cognitive value.

As a consequence of this view of meaning, philosophy would have to abandon its claim to be presenting a complete picture of reality in addition to that given by the various sciences. There may or may not be a dimension of the real which is not accessible to those disciplines. But it could not be known, or, if one might claim to have come to know it through a faculty of intellectual intuition that dispensed with sense experience, he could not express his knowledge in significant statements.[13] Any knowledge of reality as a whole would have to depend upon the piecemeal findings of the sciences.

But if philosophers could no longer pretend to be giving information about the real, what was there left for them to do? Henceforth, Ayer wrote, the task of philosophy would be the analysis of language—ordinary language, but primarily the language of science. Philosophy, that is, would have as its exclusive task the pro-

---

[12] A useful account of the membership of and influences on the Vienna Circle may be found in Victor Kraft, *The Vienna Circle,* trans. A. Pap (New York: Philosophical Library, 1953), pp. 3–11 (hereafter cited as Kraft, *Vienna*).

[13] A. J. Ayer, *Language, Truth and Logic,* 2d ed. (New York: Dover Publications, Inc., n.d.), pp. 34–35. Hereafter cited as Ayer, *Language*.

vision of definitions in use for the concepts of ordinary language and, since these were limited in difficulty and complexity and could be easily supplied, the concepts of science.[14]

By the middle of this century, then, the problems and new interests provided by developments in science, coupled with disenchantment with previous ways of doing philosophy, led English thinkers to devote their attention primarily to linguistic questions. The following positions were widely accepted:

(1) It is not the task of philosophy to provide a view of reality in opposition to, or even different from, the various sciences. Philosophy might have done so in the past; it was now agreed that this task belongs to the various special sciences.

(2) The subject matter of philosophy is language—ordinary language, and especially the language of science and mathematics.

(3) The proper method for philosophy, so understood, is analysis, conceived as a means whereby the constituents of a complex may be discovered, as a means of revealing the relationship between sense data and things, and as a means of providing definitions in use.[15]

(4) Philosophical problems arise from linguistic mistakes and misunderstandings. By means of analysis they are, or can be, successfully resolved.

It must be noted that we have not included in the above list a characteristic that many have come to associate with analytic philosophy, namely, that it is antimetaphysical. Strictly speaking, analysis is a method for the resolution of at least some philosophical problems. Those who adopt it take varying viewpoints con-

---

[14] *Ibid.,* pp. 152–153.

[15] See above, notes 5 and 6; and Ayer, *Language,* pp. 60 ff. Critical discussions and evaluations of the analytic method may be found in J. O. Urmson, *Philosophical Analysis* (Oxford: Clarendon Press, 1966); J. Hospers, *An Introduction to Philosophical Analysis* (Englewood Cliffs, N.J.: Prentice-Hall, 1953); and Samuel Gorovitz and Ron G. Williams, *Philosophical Analysis: An Introduction to Its Language and Techniques* (New York: Random House, 1965).

cerning metaphysics. Moore and Russell, for all their attacks on Bradley's idealism, were not antimetaphysical and held that the provision of a metaphysics was a highly important philosophical task.[16] The Vienna Circle, while using and advancing analytic techniques, coupled this with a radically antimetaphysical stance. But we may recall that the term *metaphysics* covers a range of variously interconnected philosophical undertakings. Positivism specifically objected to that area of metaphysical enquiry which proposed a vision of reality different from, and in fact at odds with, the views of common sense and the positive sciences. Although the later Wittgenstein believed that all philosophical problems could be resolved by dissipating the linguistic muddles from which they supposedly arose, some of his followers have been able to use his methods and technique in union with genuine metaphysical speculation. The analytic method does not, as such, require any commitment to any position vis-à-vis the possibility of metaphysics.

Logical Positivism and the Verification Principle

The view of meaning developed by positivism provided the movement with a basis for the elimination of metaphysics and the narrowing of the philosopher's interests, and permitted positivists to cast off religion and theology. Since much of the work on the nature of religious discourse has been done with this theory of meaning as a backdrop, we shall now turn to examine some of its essential features in detail.

Members of the Vienna Circle were impressed by the longevity that seems to mark so many philosophical disputes. Unlike scientific disputes, in which those involved are in general agreement as to what finding or findings would settle matters, many of the most important philosophical issues seem incapable of being laid to rest once and for all. Is reality material, spiritual, or both? This ques-

---

[16] See, for example, Bertrand Russell, "Characteristics of Mental Phenomena," Lecture 15 of *The Analysis of Mind* (London: George Allen and Unwin, Ltd., 1921), reprinted in Ammerman, *Classics*, p. 36; and G. E. Moore, *Some Main Problems of Philosophy* (London: Allen and Unwin, 1953), p. 1.

tion has been discussed in some form since pre-Socratic days. But though the participants in the debate all occupy the same world and have access to the same facts, the question is never answered to the satisfaction of all. Philosophers still remain divided on this most fundamental question. A result of this is that philosophy has made little progress in the many centuries since it began. If one compared the state of philosophical knowledge to that of knowledge in mathematics or the various positive sciences, one would realize that these disciplines had far outstripped philosophy both in the progress they had made and the progress they seemed capable of yet making. The members of the Vienna Circle believed that this state of affairs was due to philosophy itself; it was burdened with many statements that were not so much false as they were meaningless.

The word *meaningless* has a variety of meanings. For example, "Brilluns wolly jibbers" is meaningless because it is made up of nonsense words. But "Julius Caesar is a prime number," even though made up of words in current usage, is also meaningless. The reason for this is that the statement describes a real being (Caesar) in terms properly used only in reference to mathematical entities.

While the logical positivists allowed that one might find isolated instances of the above kinds of statements in some philosophical writings, they believed that the meaningless statements dangerous to philosophy were of a different kind: they appeared to be meaningful but were, in fact, meaningless. A simple example might clarify this point. Suppose someone were to say, "Every table in the universe expands at the rate of two inches per second." We can easily imagine various checking procedures that would show whether the assertion is true or false.

However, suppose someone were to say, "Everything in the universe expands at the rate of two inches per second." This statement is made up of words in current usage, there is no obvious category violation, and it is grammatically similar to the first statement. But if everything (including the speed of light) expands at the rate of two inches per second, there would be no way to judge whether this is true or false, since there is no nonexpanding standard by means of which the assertion could be checked. The first statement possesses a feature that, for all its grammatical similarity, the second statement lacks: there are means for discovering whether it is true or false. In short, it is *verifiable*.

The members of the Vienna Circle came to take verifiability as at least a necessary condition for a statement—*any* statement—to be considered meaningful. This view was expressed in the various formulations of a criterion of meaning, the verification principle, the first version of which was presented by Moritz Schlick. It stated that:

> *A statement is meaningful if and only if there are sense observations of a public kind which could finally and conclusively prove the statement's truth or falsity.*[17]

This became known as the strong version of the criterion, and it was subjected almost immediately to devastating criticism. Its major defect was that it ultimately entailed the view that all scientific laws are meaningless. A scientific law is a general or universal statement which is designed to apply to an indefinite number of cases. As such, no finite series of confirmations could ever establish its truth in a conclusive manner. For example, "A body tends to expand when heated" is always corrigible, since it must be held open to refinement, correction, and even (though it might be hard to imagine the circumstances under which this might occur) rejection. Consequently, no finite number of cases of bodies expanding when heated could *conclusively* establish this general statement. Schlick's strong formulation of the verification principle thus threw out the baby with the bathwater, since it excluded meaninglessness (and metaphysics) from the world of cognitive discourse while also excising all general or universal statements, and with them all scientific laws.[18]

---

[17] This is my own rendering of Schlick's version, as given in his "Die Kausalität in der gegenwärtigen Physik," *Die Naturwissenschaften*, XIX (1931), p. 150.

[18] This is Ayer's criticism, in Ayer, *Language*, p. 37.

Clearly, another version of the meaning criterion seemed required which would exclude meaningless statements but not general statements as such. This other formulation, the weak version, was proposed by Rudolf Carnap and A. J. Ayer. It stated that:

> *A statement is meaningful if and only if there are sense observations of a public kind that would be relevant to the truth or falsity of the statement.*[19]

Unlike the strong version, this form of the principle does not exclude general statements. For it does not require, as a condition for meaningfulness, conclusive evidence for the truth or falsity of an assertion. It makes the more moderate claim that there must be empirical observations that would tend to lead to the acceptance of the statement as true, or rejection of it as false, as a condition for considering the statement to be literally meaningful.

Though the weak version does not, therefore, exclude general statements, it is not immediately clear what else it may or may not exclude. To get a better idea of what positivism was up to at this point, we will now examine certain key conceptions that are operative behind this view of meaning.

(1) *The notion of "statement."* The Vienna Circle distinguished between two kinds of statements: the analytic and the synthetic (empirical).[20] An analytic statement is one whose predicate is contained in or implied by the subject, for example, "Every brother is a male sibling." This statement tells us nothing about the world, since to know that all brothers are male siblings is not to know whether there are any brothers, any males, or any siblings in the world. All we know is that the terms *brother* and *male sibling* are

---

[19] This is my own rendering of Ayer's version. Cf. Ayer, *Language,* pp. 36–37. See also Rudolf Carnap, *Philosophy and Logical Syntax* (London: Kegan Paul, Trench, Trubner and Co. Ltd., 1935), pp. 10 ff. (hereafter cited as Carnap, *Philosophy*).

[20] In the positivist vocabulary, a *sentence* is any grammatically significant group of words. A grammatically significant group of words that appears to assert a fact is a *statement,* an *indicative sentence,* or an *assertion.* One that does assert a fact is a *proposition;* one that does not, while appearing to do so, is a *pseudo-proposition.* Not all positivists use the above terms in strictest senses. For purposes of clarity, we shall use them henceforth as here defined. Cf. Ayer, *Language,* p. 8.

equivalent in English, so that whenever the word *brother* is used in a sentence, the words *male sibling* may be substituted for it, and vice versa. Since an analytic statement tells us nothing about the world, its truth or falsity is not affected by any empirical state of affairs, but is decided by the going linguistic conventions. Analytic statements, even though without factual value, are nevertheless important, since they help us clarify the meanings of terms or understand more fully how language works.[21]

A synthetic statement is one in which the predicate is not contained in, or implied by, the subject, for example, "All teachers are inspiring." It alleges to tell us something about the world, and its truth or falsity must consequently depend on how things are in the world. It is always corrigible, that is, open to correction or revision if future observations require this. I may have no good reason at present to doubt the truth of the statement "There is a typewriter in front of me," but there are conceivable circumstances (a future discovery that I was hallucinating when I made the statement, for example) which, should they occur, would lead me to question it. Because it is always corrigible, a synthetic statement can never be certain. A statement that is certain (and analytic statements alone can be such) is one whose falsity is impossible, that is, whose denial would involve a self-contradiction. No matter how good the evidence might be for any synthetic statement, its denial is never self-contradictory. For this reason, a synthetic statement can be only highly probable at best.[22]

---

[21] Moritz Schlick, *Problems of Ethics,* trans. D. Rynin (New York: Prentice-Hall Inc., 1939), p. 109; Ayer, *Language,* pp. 78–80; and Rudolf Carnap, *Introduction to Semantics* and *Formalization of Logic* (Cambridge: Harvard University Press, 1959), p. 141.

[22] The only exception to this is the *protocol, observation,* or *basic* statement which refers to the content of a single experience, for example, "I am seeing a red patch now." It is certain that I am seeing a red patch now, whether or not there is a red patch in front of me to be seen. The statement does not claim that others can see it, and future events could not lead me to reject the statement. As a result, the observation statement conveys no information whatever to anyone. No synthetic statements which convey information can be certain. Cf. Ayer, *Language,* pp. 10–11. See also Rudolf Carnap, *The Unity of Science,* trans. M. Black (London: Kegan Paul, Trench, Trubner and Co. Ltd., 1934), pp. 44–45.

The verification principle was not designed to deal with analytic statements, whose truth or falsity could be decided by relatively easy means. At any rate, the problems of philosophy did not arise from false or badly worded analytic statements. Rather, the verification principle was proposed in order to deal with synthetic statements by dividing them into two classes: the meaningful and the meaningless. Only meaningful statements could really tell us something about the world, and the verification principle sought to discover, for any given synthetic statement, whether it accomplished this function.

(2) *The notion of "public sense observation."* The kind of observation or experience in terms of which positivism held synthetic statements to be meaningful was of a public kind, that is, of a kind that is open, *in principle,* to anyone wishing to have it. If an individual claimed to have had a unique kind of experience in which others could not share—a mystical vision, for example—he could not then communicate that experience to anyone else. Those to whom he spoke would lack any similar experience in terms of which what was said to them could be understood. Though rich in metaphor and imagery and capable of conveying powerful feelings, statements that refer to *sui generis* experience are devoid of literal significance. This last property belongs to those statements, and those statements alone, that refer to matters that can be observed by others.

Such matters, however, need be open to others only *in principle.* There might be observations that, in fact, I alone make. Suppose, for instance, I am alone in a room and a book falls off a table. In a sense this is a private experience, since I alone have observed it. Is the statement "The book fell off the table" then meaningless? No, for the event referred to is of a kind that is observable by others. That I alone happened to be in the room does not alter the character of the event as one that is, so to speak, in the public domain.[23]

---

[23] Ayer, *Language,* p. 97. Note also the demand that underlies Ayer's discussion of basic statements, that the verifying experience be, in principle, of a public kind (p. 10). There is a similar demand for historical statements (p. 19).

(3) *The various kinds of verifiability.* The verification principle connected the notions of meaningfulness and empirical verifiability. How, precisely, is the latter notion to be understood? It is clear that "Pine trees have leaves in the winter" is a verifiable assertion. But since the statement "There are approximately 10,000 genes in a human chromosome" speaks of theoretical entities whose existence cannot be sensed, is it verifiable? Again, "Water boils at 100° C" is verifiable, but in the absence of available means of learning whether the statement might be true or false, is the statement "There are diamonds on Pluto" verifiable?

In order to deal with these questions, positivists distinguished between direct and indirect verification, and between verifiability in fact, or practical verifiability, and verifiability in principle.[24] A statement is said to be directly verifiable if (1) it is an "observation statement," or (2) it is such that, in conjunction with one or more observation statements it entails another observation statement which is not deducible from these other statements alone. Thus, "Either my pen is black or my typewriter is blue" is directly verifiable, since together with "My pen is black" it entails "My typewriter is not blue." Some statements are not directly verifiable but only indirectly so. A statement is said to be indirectly verifiable if, in conjunction with other premises, it entails at least one directly verifiable statement which is not deducible from the other premises alone; and each of the premises must be either analytic or directly verifiable, or at least capable of being independently established as indirectly verifiable. "This key is made of iron" is indirectly verifiable since, when taken with "I am putting this key near to a magnet," the directly verifiable statement "This key will stick to the magnet" is deducible.[25]

A statement is said to be verifiable in fact if we can actually perform the relevant tests or can have the necessary experiences

[24] Carnap, *Philosophy,* pp. 10–13; Ayer, *Language,* pp. 36, 39. See also Herbert Feigl, "Logical Empiricism," in H. Feigl and W. Sellars, eds., *Readings in Philosophical Analysis* (New York: Appleton-Century-Crofts, Inc., 1949), p. 10 (This collection hereafter cited as Feigl, *Readings.*)
[25] Carnap, *Philosophy,* pp. 11–12; Ayer, *Language,* pp. 11–13.

which would have a bearing on the statement's truth-value. But a statement is verifiable in principle if the actual or practical means for verification are lacking. Hence, since we have available the means for verification, "Water boils at 100° C" is verifiable in fact; but in the absence of technical know-how, "There are diamonds on Pluto" is verifiable in principle.

Positivism did not wish to exclude statements that were verifiable in principle from the class of the meaningful, since their not being verifiable in fact was not the result of some inherent defect in them but was, rather, a matter of the relative state of human knowledge and capabilities. Besides, to restrict meaningfulness in this way would place an intolerable limit on the scope of scientific investigation. Many important statements, though not factually verifiable, still have valuable cognitive and scientific functions to perform.

While there was some difficulty in specifying the exact limits of the notion of verification in principle,[26] there was unanimity among the members of the Vienna Circle that there was a certain class of statement that was not verifiable in any way and could therefore be ignored as meaningless: those statements which no experience could either confirm or disconfirm, render true or false.

What was the status of such meaningless assertions? Although tossing them, one and all, in the "emotive" category,[27] positivists were careful to point out that to call a statement meaningless, or emotive, was not to pass judgment on its standing in the life of the one using it. A meaningless statement might be rich in human values. It might indicate a mystical feeling towards reality without which life would be the poorer; it might have moral or aesthetic force; it might convey emotions, or have a profound effect on the one to whom it is addressed.[28] But this would not mean that it

---

[26] See, for example, Moritz Schlick, "Meaning and Verification," in Feigl, *Readings,* p. 154; G. Schlesinger, *Method in the Physical Sciences* (London: Routledge and Kegan Paul, Ltd., 1963), pp. 111, 112; and Hans Reichenbach, *Experience and Prediction* (Chicago: The University of Chicago Press, 1938), pp. 47–48.

[27] Ayer, *Language,* p. 44.

[28] *Ibid.,* p. 45.

had any "theoretical value." This depended, in the last analysis, upon whether, from the statement, any consequences that could be sensibly verified could be drawn. As Carnap expressed the view, language has a *representative* as well as an *expressive* function. A meaningful statement, although it might indicate our feelings, attitudes, and the like (its expressive side), also gives information about a state of affairs (its representative side). But a meaningless statement, though it might have an expressive function, is deficient in representative value.[29]

Meaninglessness of Ethical, Metaphysical, and Religious Statements

What kinds of statements did the verification principle exclude as meaningless? Relevant to philosophy, it excluded ethical and aesthetic judgments, metaphysical statements, and theological or religious statements.

(1) *Ethical and aesthetic judgments.*[30] Ayer distinguished four kinds of statements that could be found in the writings of ethical philosophers. They were (a) propositions expressing the definitions of ethical terms, or judgments about the possibility of certain definitions; (b) propositions describing moral experience and its causes; (c) exhortations to virtue; and (d) actual ethical judgments. Statements of the first type were the proper subject of ethics; of the second were considered the province of sociology or psychol-

---

[29] Carnap, *Philosophy,* pp. 27–29. Those who still hold to some version of the verification principle sometimes speak of the principle of *falsifiability.* This is in the wake of Karl Popper who, in *The Logic of Scientific Discovery* (London: Hutchinson and Co. Ltd., 1959) attacked the verification principle in its strong formulation on the grounds that it was based on a faulty theory of induction; he suggested a *criterion of falsifiability,* according to which a statement or system of statements is empirical and conveys information about the empirical world only if it is capable of *clashing* with experience. Those that were incapable of clashing were not, according to Popper, meaningless; they were simply not empirical. However, other thinkers have adopted Popper's falsifiability criterion as a variant of the verification principle, that is, as distinguishing between meaningful and meaningless statements. For Popper's views, see pp. 35–37, 41, 312–314, and 317. An important discussion of the vicissitudes of the criterion of meaning may be found in Carl G. Hempel, "Problems and Changes in the Empiricist Criterion of Meaning," *Révue internationale de philosophie,* IV (1950), pp. 41–62.

[30] Ayer, *Language,* pp. 102 ff.

ogy; the third kind were not really propositions at all, though they might appear so, but had the status of ejaculations or commands designed to bring about a certain course of action. Statements of the fourth kind contained normative ethical symbols—words like right, wrong, and the like; a large portion of moral philosophy is composed of such statements. But Ayer maintained that these are not statements of fact that can be true or false as many take them to be, but are merely expressions of moral sentiments. The man who says "Stealing is wrong" is stating no more than his disapproval of stealing. His statement is emotive and expresses only his feelings; it has no cognitive content. If propositions describing moral experience and its causes belong to the domain of psychology and sociology, then so do actual ethical judgments. As expressions of feeling, one can ask of them only, "What are the moral habits of a person or group of people?" and, "What causes them to have those habits and feelings?" Ethics is then reduced to the domain of the social sciences; what is left is to say that normative symbols are pseudoconcepts.

(2) *Metaphysical statements.* The term *metaphysics* is variously used, and one may find historical precedent for calling the following types of philosophical activity metaphysical: the attempt to elaborate a picture of reality as a whole; the attempt to describe a dimension of ordinary experience that escapes the various special sciences; the analysis of those concepts and principles common to all, or more than one, of the special sciences; and the examination and defense of those assumptions on which the possibility of knowledge rests. Although a great deal of the work that positivists considered proper to a reformed philosophy and which they themselves pursued, such as the analysis of scientific concepts, could be called metaphysical in some sense of that term, it is clear that the metaphysics they condemned as meaningless was that discipline which attempted to give an account of reality other than that given by the various sciences.

But what was the precise objection to a uniquely philosophical description of reality? All knowledge originates in sense experience. By what valid process, positivism asked, could a philosopher then attain a conception of reality other than, or transcending, the reality which his sense experience gave him, and which thus belonged in principle to the various special sciences? From empirical premises there can be no legitimate inference to matters transcending the empirical. But if the philosopher claimed that he knew the transcendent in a way that dispensed with sense experience, the positivist then pointed out that he was thereby forced to cut all connection between the statements that embodied his knowledge and meaningful speech.[31] Only if a statement is such that sense experience is relevant to questions of its truth or falsity can that statement be considered meaningful; and positivism believed that this was no arbitrary demand, but a consequence drawn from the very nature of language itself.

What is the function of language? In the positivist view, language has a single, essential function: to anticipate the course of our sensations, to warn us beforehand what our experience will be.[32] If, indeed, this is the essential function of language, it then follows that a statement which does not anticipate experience tells us nothing. It is a pseudoproposition; it fails to fulfill language's essential purpose; it is meaningless. The metaphysician thus finds himself in a quandary. Either his understanding of reality is drawn from experience and gives information about experience; or, gained by nonsensual means, it tells us nothing about experience. If the former, then what is said falls within the actual or possible scope of one or the other of the sciences. If the latter, his statements have nothing to say about the world and are therefore meaningless.

(3) *Theological or religious statements.*[33] Christian believers hold that there are certain truths they know that, without God's revelation of himself to man, they might not otherwise have known. They know, for example, that there is a God, that he is good and providentially cares for the world. But since these statements and others like them refer to a being who transcends expe-

---

[31] *Ibid.*, pp. 33–34.
[32] *Ibid.*, pp. 97, 99.
[33] *Ibid.*, pp. 114 ff.

rience, they are metaphysical statements and, as such, are meaning-less. The same reasons advanced against metaphysics are therefore operative against theology. However, because of the importance of this point in our study, we will examine it in further detail.

Can it be shown through rational demonstration that the statement "God exists" is true? There is the general requirement that in any reasoning process the conclusion can be no stronger than the premises which support it. If "God exists" is demonstrated as certain, it must be supported by premises that are themselves certain. But as certainty is a property of analytic statements alone, and as empirical statements can be only probable, it follows that if a demonstration for God's existence begins with empirical premises, the conclusion of the demonstration can itself be only probable. Nor can the existence of God be deduced from true analytic statements alone. From a tautology only a tautology follows. Once again, the conclusion can state no more than the premises warrant; and if the premises do not bear on matters of fact, the conclusion cannot do so, as, supposedly, "God exists" does.[34]

The heart of Ayer's position, however, and its characteristically positivist flavor, lies in his view that "God exists" cannot even be probable. It is not that the evidence which may be cited in its favor does not allow it to be called "probable," but that from "God exists" no experiential proposition can be deduced. "God exists" is therefore a meaningless assertion.[35]

To know that God exists is not to be able to predict that certain events will or will not occur. Theist and atheist both inhabit the same world, and their respective views on God's existence do not alter their expectations of experience. It might be true that some theists hold that regularity and order in nature provide sufficient evidence for the existence of God. But to say "God exists" is to say more than "There are regularities in nature." The theist wishes his statement to be grounded in the experience of such regularities, but to transcend them. But then "God exists" reveals itself as a metaphysical assertion, since it goes beyond experience

---

[34] *Ibid.*, pp. 114–115.
[35] *Ibid.*, p. 115.

or experiential confirmation. This is why, Ayer concludes, the positivist position must be distinguished from both atheistic and agnostic stances. The atheist holds that "God exists" is false; the agnostic sees no evidence to support either the truth or falsity of the statement. But both these positions imply that "God exists" is a meaningful assertion. This, however, is precisely what positivism denies.[36]

Objections to Positivism

The verificationist view of meaning has been subjected to a great deal of detailed criticism. It has proved remarkably resilient, adapting and changing under attacks from various sides while still preserving the fundamental idea that language in general required any statement claiming meaningfulness to be sensibly verifiable. Nevertheless, many thinkers, including some who were originally associated with the Vienna Circle, became dissatisfied with that group's univocal approach to this problem, especially since it involved using the definition of meaningfulness as an executioner's sword to destroy whole areas of human discourse. There were various focuses of dissatisfaction, not all of them of equal merit. Some were more damaging to the positivist program than others; some were answered by means of further refinement and clarification of the positions involved; some were less successful than their proponents had hoped. Some of the objections most often levelled against the positivist criterion of meaning follow.

(1) The verification principle is not an analytic statement—not, that is, a conception of meaningfulness that is true by definition. It is a synthetic statement. As such, there would have to be sense experience relevant to its truth-value if it is to be itself considered meaningful. But there is no sense experience that could conceivably show the principle to be either true or false. The verification principle thus implies its own meaninglessness.

This objection is answered by pointing out that the verification principle is a rule that specifies the characteristics necessary for lan-

---

[36] *Ibid.*, pp. 115–116.

guage that speaks about factual matters. It does not, consequently, have to conform to the rule that it lays down. To amplify: there are levels of language, and language may be used at one level to lay down a rule for language at another level which it, itself, does not obey. The verification principle states a rule for what may be called "first level language," that is, language that alleges to speak about factual matters. But the principle is a bit of second level language, since it does not claim to be speaking about a factual matter, but only about the characteristics a first level language ought to have if it is to accomplish its essential purpose.

(2) There are, in common usage, many meanings of the word *meaningful*. The verification principle has selected one of these, in which "to be meaningful" is equivalent with "to have sense consequences." But this is arbitrary. While there is a sense of being meaningful which is as the verification principle states, there is no warrant to select this particular meaning and make it a norm for language in general.

This criticism fails to give sufficient weight to the reason why the Vienna Circle chose from all possible meanings of the term *meaningful,* the one it did. It was because language was conceived as having but one essential purpose, the anticipation of experience. There might be other functions in addition to this, the Circle agreed, but this is the essential one that underlies, or ought to underlie, all others. Consequently, the verification principle asks that, whatever else a statement may do, it fulfill the minimum condition of experience-prediction as a condition for meaningfulness.

In addition to the above objections, there are others that are somewhat more successful in pointing up inadequacies in and some unstated assumptions behind the positivist conception of meaning. None of these, however, meets what appears to be the primary issue here, whether or not language has but a single essential function.

(3) A sign (word, sentence) is meaningless only when nothing has been coordinated with it by stipulation. Since different rules may be stipulated for the same sign, a sentence which is meaningless in one language may be meaningful in another which has dif-

ferent semantic and syntactic constructions. The syntactic rules of one language may, for example, forbid the predication of psychological terms to inorganic entities, with the result that "The sky is laughing" would be considered meaningless. The rules of another language may allow the word *laughing* to designate not a mental state, but the power of causing a mental state. "The sky is laughing" would, in that language, then be meaningful. It is therefore impossible to distinguish one class of statement from another by calling one meaningful and the other meaningless. Since the meaning of a statement depends on the structure of the language in which it functions, it is possible to construct a semantic system in which even metaphysical statements are meaningful. The mistake made by positivism lies in the attempt made to separate metaphysics from science on the basis of an absolute conception of language. But there are many possible languages, and from these the language of *empiricism* selects one that satisfies the following rules: (a) reducibility of the meaning of descriptive signs to ostentation of what those signs designate in experience; and (b) empirical testability of a factual assertion, which means the ultimate possibility of pointing to the experiential data that supports it. The language of a transcendental metaphysics will not conform to the rules of this empirical language (and is thereby distinguishable from scientific language), and will, in terms of *that* language, be unverifiable and meaningless. But as there exists more than one language, it cannot be claimed that the language of metaphysics is, without qualification, meaningless. An empirical criterion of meaning does not, as positivists seem to think, result from the conditions of language in general, but is instead the criterion of one special language.[37]

(4) The verification principle is a normative rule, since it makes a proposal for the use of language. Its only adequate defense must, however, bring in an arbitrary assumption, namely, that the way an empirical assertion "faces" evidence is normative for all assertions which may be considered meaningful. Now while

---

[37] This is Kraft's objection, in *Vienna,* pp. 40–41.

it might be true that most of our knowledge has a certain characteristic, for example, that it stands or falls before empirical evidence, we cannot on that basis argue that all our knowledge must
have this characteristic. In fact, we must expect that knowledge of
transcendent entities, if we have such knowledge, would possess
characteristics different from knowledge of things met with in ordinary experience. One area of knowledge, or knowledge of one
kind of being, cannot provide a base from which we can successfully rule out the possibility of another area of knowledge, or
knowledge of another kind of being.[38]

(5) Finally, the most successful objection argued that the way
positivism understood the concept of empirical verifiability was
faulty, since it would allow *any* statement whatever to be meaningful. While this objection was directed specifically against
Ayer's understanding of empirical verifiability as given in the introduction to the second edition of *Language, Truth and Logic,* it
has led many thinkers to conclude that it is not possible to construct a formulation of that concept that would allow meaningless
statements to be distinguished from meaningful ones.[39] The argument goes as follows:

Let *p, q,* and *r* be three observation statements such that no one
of them alone entails any of the others. Using these, we may show
that any statement, *S,* or its negation $(-S)$ is verifiable. Consider
the following arguments:

1. $(-p \cdot q) \vee (r \cdot -S)$ premise
2. p premise

---

[38] This is a conflation of various criticisms urged by, among others, Alfred
C. Ewing, "Religious Assertions in the Light of Contemporary Philosophy,"
Philosophy, XXXII (1957), pp. 206–218; Maxwell J. Charlesworth, "Linguistic Analysis and Language About God," *International Philosophical Quarterly,* I (1961), pp. 139 ff.; and John E. Smith's contribution to "Symposium:
The Present Status of Natural Theology," *The Journal of Philosophy,* LV
(1958), pp. 925–944.

[39] However, Wesley C. Salmon is "optimistic" about the possibility of constructing a satisfactory meaning criterion. See his "Verifiability and Logic,"
Paul K. Feyerabend and Grover Maxwell, eds., *Mind, Matter, and Method*
(Minneapolis, Minn.: University of Minnesota Press, 1966), pp. 354–376
(hereafter cited as Feyerabend, *Mind*).

3. $((-p \cdot q) \vee r) \cdot ((-p \cdot q) \vee -S)$ 1. distribution
4. $(-p \cdot q) \vee r$ 3. simplification
5. $(-p \vee r) \cdot (q \vee r)$ 4. distribution
6. $-p \vee r$ 5. simplification
7. r 2., 6. disjunctive argument

According to Ayer's definition of direct verifiability (see pp. 20–24), this argument shows that premise 1 is directly verifiable.

1. $(-p \cdot q) \vee (r \cdot -S)$ premise
2. S premise
3. $(-p \vee (r \cdot -S)) \cdot (q \vee (r \cdot -S))$ 1. distribution
4. $(q \vee r) \cdot (q \vee -S)$ 3. simplification & distribution
5. $q \vee -S$ 4. simplification
6. q 2, 5. disjunctive argument

Now either (a) the first premise of the above two arguments alone entails q, or, (b) the first premise of the above two arguments does not alone entail q. Let us suppose (a). Then, $((-p \cdot q) \vee (r \cdot -S))$ entails q and $(r \cdot -S)$ entails q. Therefore, according to Ayer's explication, $-S$ is directly verifiable.

Let us suppose (b). Then, since $(-p \cdot q) \vee (r \cdot -S)$ is directly verifiable, it follows from the second argument that S is indirectly verifiable.

Therefore, according to Ayer's explication, either S or $-S$ is literally meaningful. But since if a statement is meaningful its denial is meaningful as well, and vice versa, it follows that both S and $-S$ are literally meaningful.[40]

Wittgenstein's Later Theory of Meaning

Death from wounds inflicted by frontal assault is seldom the fate of philosophical theories. They are more often abandoned,

---

[40] Alonzo Church, "Review of Ayer's *Language, Truth and Logic*," *Journal of Symbolic Logic*, XIV (1949), pp. 52–53. I am grateful to Dr. John Vollrath of Purdue University at Fort Wayne for this explication of Church's argument.

usually because they either fail to live up to early promises, or because the emergence of new and different interests is not consonant with them. Despite the objections levelled against it, the positivist conception of meaningfulness did not, and has not, completely surrendered the field. But by the early 1950's, philosophers began moving toward another, more flexible theory of language. The basic dissatisfaction with the one positivism taught was that it placed a stranglehold on language that only a few areas of discourse escaped. All the rest was meaningless. This restricted philosophers far more than many were willing to permit. Especially when more patient analyses of the emotive areas of language revealed nuances which positivism was unwilling to take seriously, thinkers became receptive to a theory of language that allowed detailed investigation into *all* areas of language, without deciding issues in advance by blanket discussions of meaningfulness and its opposite. In short, positivism limned with broad strokes in black and white; thinkers needed a finer brush, and colors that would reflect refinement and variety of tone, in order to speak fully about human discourse.

In his *Tractatus,* Wittgenstein had been struck by the similarity between a statement and its relationship to facts, and a picture and its relationship to a scene that it depicts. He used the latter as a workable model by means of which the former could be understood. As a picture gives knowledge of a scene, so language gives knowledge of reality; as a picture might show detail in varying degrees, so language could represent reality in similar degrees; as a picture might be said to function mainly by depicting a scene, so language has its essential function in depicting reality. This theory, shared by other thinkers as well (Russell, for example, and to a large extent, various positivists), Wittgenstein came to believe to be an invention foisted on language rather than a discovery of some essential element in it.[41] In 1952, the year after his death,

---

[41] Ludwig Wittgenstein, *Philosophical Investigations,* trans. G. E. M. Anscombe (New York: The Macmillan Company, 1953), I, 107, 112 ff. This work is made up of a series of numbered paragraphs to which the cited numbers refer. Hereafter cited as Wittgenstein, *Investigations.* There are a number of

his *Philosophical Investigations* was published, in which *tools* and *games* were suggested as models for understanding language.

If we look at language as it is actually used, Wittgenstein wrote, we are immediately struck by the many functions it performs. We use language to achieve different ends: to describe an event, to compliment someone, to pray, to express a desire, to comfort, to advise, to reassure, to suggest a course of action, to make excuses, to warn, to interpret events, to make promises, to reveal our feelings and attitudes, to praise, to blame, to speculate about an event.[42] But isn't there some single function that subtends all of these? Wittgenstein came to believe that those who thought so had not based their opinion on a detailed canvass of *all* language-uses. Rather, they had decided that language had, and even *had* to have, a certain primary function, such as the picturing of facts, and *then* had proceeded to investigate language with this idea in mind. It might be, of course, that language does have a primary purpose to fulfill, or is related to facts in the way that a picture is related to the scene it depicts. But this discovery would have to be founded on a survey of *all* actual language-uses, not just on a few important ones, and could not be decided prior to investigation. However, given a multi-functioned language, the discovery of language's essential function—if it has one—would not particularly help us to understand how any specific bit of language actually functions.

Wittgenstein found that the model of tools in a toolbox, each having a different job to perform, provided a richer and more complete model for the understanding of language than the picture theory did.[43] Do all tools have a single, essential function? We cannot assume that they do. We must look and see, and resist the temptation to assume that they must because we give them the

---

excellent studies dealing with Wittgenstein and his work. A recent, and highly readable, essay on his overall intellectual development is Stephen Toulmin, "Ludwig Wittgenstein," *Encounter,* XXXII, no. 1 (January, 1969), pp. 58–71.

[42] Wittgenstein, *Investigations,* I, 23, 24.

[43] *Ibid.,* I, 11. See also the model of a city's streets which Wittgenstein suggests to provide a model whereby the development of language may be understood. *Ibid.,* I, 18.

common name, "tools." A survey of tools that an average home-
owner may have would be enough to show us that any definition we might frame which would include them all—that they all
serve to modify something, for example—would probably not
meet minimal criteria for a good definition, and in any case would
not help us to know what could or could not be done with any
specific tool. To say that an adz modifies something says nothing
about what it may be used to do or the manner of its employment.
It is in its particular usefulness, moreover, that its value and *rai-
son d'etre* are found.[44]

As the value of a tool lies in what may be done with it, so the
value of a sentence, its meaning, is often a function of its use: who
is using it, to whom it is addressed, in what context, and to attain
what end. As a description of what all tools might have in
common—their essential "toolness", so to speak—does not tell us
how any individual tool might work, so a general description that
might cover all language-functions might say nothing about how
an individual bit of language might work. To see language on the
model of tools is to set aside the search for a feature common to
all language and to look instead for the concrete, specific use(s) to
which a sentence might be put.

Games provided Wittgenstein with another model by means of
which language might be better understood.[45] Once again, some
general description of what all games might have in common, even
if it could be framed, would probably tell us nothing about the
rules, moves, and objectives of an individual game. These could be
learned only on a piecemeal basis, just as the specific uses of language could be learned only in a similar manner and could not be
gleaned from some general description that supposedly covered all
instances. But the game model provided Wittgenstein with a further insight into language. As there are various games, each differing to some degree from all others but all connected by a host
of interwoven likenesses, so there are various languages, each differing from every other but all nevertheless connected by a network

---

[44] *Ibid.*, I, 14.
[45] *Ibid.*, I, 66.

of intertwining similarities. Although it would be difficult to find some single element common to football, chess, tennis, squash, bridge, poker, checkers, handball, baseball, cricket, and solitaire, they nevertheless exhibit "family resemblances" and are grouped by us into that class of activities we call games.[46] The elements that make tennis similar to squash are not those that make tennis similar to baseball, and the elements that differentiate solitaire from chess may not differentiate chess from bridge. In like manner, the languages of advice-giving, description, joke-telling, action-justification, praise, and blame possess no single common element, but exhibit varying kinds of family resemblances and are grouped by us into that wide family of activities we call language. It is this parallel between language and games that Wittgenstein had in mind when he spoke of "language-games." [47] This term does not imply that there is something trivial or unimportant about language—Wittgenstein referred to it as "a form of life" [48]—but is intended as a reminder that the languages we use are as various as the games we play. Each has its own rules, moves, and objectives, and are like and unlike each other in differing degrees and often in terms of differing elements.

As we cannot justifiably claim that there is any ideal or paradigmatic game which represents a standard for judging whether to call a particular activity a game, Wittgenstein denied that there was any normative language-game against which other language-games could be measured and judged. A given linguistic move might be forbidden by the rules of one language-game (as, analogously, a move might be forbidden in one board game), but permitted by another. For example, the language of personal relationships may allow statements to be used in order to evoke a personal response from the one addressed, whereas the language of positive science may make no room for such statement functions. A consequence of this is that the terms *meaningful* and *meaningless* cannot be defined in an absolute or normative sense,

---

[46] *Ibid.*, I, 67.
[47] *Ibid.*, I, 23, 67.
[48] *Ibid.*, I, 23.

but will have various meanings depending on the language-game in which they operate.

In brief, Wittgenstein's later view of language involves the following features:

(1) The functions of language are many and various. The sentences we use are as different in purpose as the tools in a toolbox. If language has a primary function, this can be discovered only after all the uses of language have been explored. Furthermore, knowing this primary function would probably not help us in knowing the specific way in which a particular bit of language is to be used.

(2) As seen in terms of the game model, language is an interconnected series of activities, each with its own rules, moves, and objectives. These will differ in varying degrees from language to language.

(3) No single language, or function of language, is normative for all others. Each language-game is a form of life, to be understood on its own merits and in terms of its individual characteristics. No language-game can be condemned because of its failure to measure up to the requirements of some other language-game.

Wittgenstein and Religious Language

In none of Wittgenstein's major works is extensive attention paid to religious language and belief. Student notes on his lectures in this area were published in 1966,[49] but they are sketchy in the extreme and reveal Wittgenstein surveying, almost groping through, a broad range of topics rather than investigating any particular issue in depth. Among matters touched upon are Christianity and history, the nature of religious belief and its differences from other kinds of belief, the relationship between miracles and faith, the way the meaning of the word *God* is learned, faith and rationality, and how we come to understand the content of a religious statement. A brief look at a couple of these topics might prove of interest.

(1) *The nature of religious belief.* Religious and scientific be-

---

[49] Ludwig Wittgenstein, *Lectures and Conversations on Aesthetics, Psychology, and Religious Belief,* ed. Cyril Barrett (Oxford: Basil Blackwell, 1966).

liefs differ not only in their respective relationships to facts, but even in the language we use when speaking about them. We speak of "dogma" and "faith" in the context of religious belief, but of "high probability" and "hypothesis" with reference to scientific belief.[50] Religious belief seems, in part at least, to perform a *regulative* function in the life of the believer, in that he acts and takes risks because of it.[51] It is *interpretive* as well, because by means of it he thinks of things in distinctive ways (sickness, for instance, in terms of retribution).[52] To have a religious belief, as in a final judgment after death, is to have a focus where "a number of ways of thinking and acting crystallize and come together." [53] Wittgenstein seems to have been struck by the way religious beliefs are associated with pictures. The believer, he suggested, might justify his actions by "appealing to this picture" (the Last Judgment),[54] and differs from the nonbeliever in that he has "different pictures." [55] Belief in dogmas like God's creation of man are connected with pictures [56] (Michelangelo's paintings, for example); even religious statements ("God's eye sees everything") might involve pictures having different degrees of importance in the language and life of the believer.[57]

(2) *Religious language.* Wittgenstein spoke of religious language in terms of his game theory, and suggested that a statement may not possess its religious character by virtue of what it's about, but rather from the total context in which it operates. A religious assertion, or belief, has "entirely different connections" [58] from a scientific assertion, even though we could easily imagine instances in which we would not know whether we were dealing with a religious or a scientific tenet. How do we learn the meaning of a religious statement like "My idea of death is the separation of soul and body"? We could do so by asking what consequences this be-

---

[50] *Ibid.*, p. 57.
[51] *Ibid.*, pp. 53, 54.
[52] *Ibid.*, pp. 54–55.
[53] *Ibid.*, p. 56.
[54] *Ibid.*, p. 54.
[55] *Ibid.*, p. 55.
[56] *Ibid.*, p. 63.
[57] *Ibid.*, p. 71.
[58] *Ibid.*, p. 58.

lief might have, by seeing what the believer opposes to this belief
—(that he ceased to be entirely after death, for example) or by
discovering what is connected with it (ideas of an afterlife of joy
or suffering, ideas of ethical responsibility).[59] But Wittgenstein
sensed the problematic and difficult character of religious statements. Religious controversies, he judged, "look quite different
from any normal controversies" (including scientific ones), and
reasons cited in favor of one side or another "look entirely different from normal reasons." [60] They are "quite inconclusive," and if
evidence of a scientific kind were involved "this would in fact destroy the whole business." [61] It is not surprising to find him puz-
zled by the linguistic moves in religious controversies (and, no
doubt, in religious language generally), and to find him claiming
that they disrupt his "normal technique of language." [62]

However, if Wittgenstein's own work in the philosophy of religion is tentative and in bare outline, analytic philosophers found
his later theory of language useful in providing a fresh understanding of religious discourse. Consequently, the following methodological procedures and assumptions have come to be widely
adopted.

(1) The meaning of a religious statement is seen in the use that
is made of it, and we cannot determine in advance of a close scrutiny of its actual use(s) what it may mean. So, for example, "God
loves man" may be used in a relatively simple way (to comfort
someone) or in a highly complicated manner (in the context of a
theology lecture). Differences in statement-usage could involve differences in statement-meanings.

(2) Discussions of religious assertions are not to be conducted
within the context of an inflexible and absolute understanding of
meaningfulness. Instead, emphasis is placed on the description of
the functions, purposes, and objectives of religious language and
its relationship to other language-games.

(3) It is probable that the language of religion is similar in some

[59] *Ibid.*, pp. 69–70.
[60] *Ibid.*, p. 56.
[61] *Ibid.*
[62] *Ibid.*, p. 55.

respects to other language-games. But this does not necessarily imply that religious discourse can be reduced *in toto* to some other language or group of languages. Examination may reveal that it has some irreducible element or even elements, all of which are found in other languages but are present here in some unique, differentiating combination. But such matters cannot be decided in advance of a canvass of all the types of religious uses of language.

(4) It is possible that religious language is a collection, or "family," of languages. That is, it may include ethical or moral language, the language of attitude formation and expression, the language of personal commitment, and others, and these may have different values and standings in the life of believers. We cannot assume that there is a single feature involved in all religious uses of language which accounts for their religious nature. There may be a number of characteristics, "a complicated net-work of similarities overlapping and criss-crossing." [63]

Summary

Developments in the physical sciences, together with a growing lack of interest in the then-prevalent style of philosophizing, led English philosophers in this century to devote their attention to the problems raised by ordinary, scientific, and mathematical language. The technique of analysis was developed as a means of handling these problems. The school of logical positivism expressed its understanding of language and meaning in terms of the verification principle, which proposed that meaningfulness was a property possessed only by those statements that can be verified in terms of sense experience. Metaphysical and religious assertions were declared to be noncognitive and could therefore be ignored. During the past two decades, however, the less rigid conception of language proposed by Ludwig Wittgenstein in his *Philosophical Investigations* has had increasing influence. It has affected the approach that philosophers could take to religious language, allowing it to be explored in a more flexible and sympathetic manner.

----

[63] Wittgenstein, *Investigations*, I, 66. For further discussion of the Wittgensteinian approach to religious language, see Jerry H. Gill, "Wittgenstein and Religious Language," *Theology Today*, XXI (1964), pp. 59–72.

III

The Meaning of
Religious Statements

Were one deity antecedently proved by your theory, who were possessed of every attribute, requisite to the production of the universe; it would be needless, I own . . . to suppose any other deity existent. But while it is still a question, whether all these attributes are united in one subject, or dispersed among several independent beings: by what phenomena in nature can we pretend to decide the controversy?

David Hume, *Dialogues Concerning Natural Religion*, V.

Philosophy is a battle against the bewitchment of our intelligence by means of language.

Ludwig Wittgenstein, *Philosophical Investigations*, I, 109.

Introduction

The analytic method does not commit the one using it to any specific stand on questions such as the ultimate nature of reality or the limits of knowledge. Plato may find it a valuable tool no less than Aristotle, and, indeed, some of its contemporary employers profess their complete freedom from all epistemological and metaphysical beliefs. As we saw in the last chapter, however, analysis grew up alongside diverse theories of language and meaning. While as a technique it is neutral to them all, what it is allowed to reveal is frequently determined by the stands taken on these matters by the individual philosopher using it. One who holds that all talk of the transcendent is nonsensical finds analysis revealing only attitudes or feelings at the heart of religious assertions, while another whose positions in this area are less constrictive might find

42

analysis helpful in isolating and characterizing the knowledge-content which believers insist is present in at least some of their uses of religious assertions.

It was not long after the publication of *Language, Truth and Logic* that writers found it necessary to go beyond the "emotive" category that positivism had erected as a catch-all for important but alleged nonsignificant statements, and to try to chart the precise functions of religious statements in the lives of believers. Two features characterized much of this early work. First, it was notoriously reductionist, as writer followed writer in presenting what was taken to be the only, or one central, task for religious language. Second, these explorations were undertaken on the tacit, and occasionally explicit, assumption that religious statements had no cognitive value. Since the early 1950s, however, and under the influence of Wittgenstein's later conception of language, the bases for work in this area have gradually changed, even though use of the common analytic method accounts for some similarities between more recent explorations and earlier ones. The majority of philosophers today are receptive to the idea that there is not, and does not have to be, any single task that religious language performs, that it has different but interrelated functions. Instead of broad and overly simple investigations, they now attend to particular statement-types, or statement-uses, careful that their conclusions be no wider than the data on which they are based. Finally, many consider the positivists' meaningful/meaningless categories as irrelevant and misleading, or at least subject them to intensive criticism before using them. The going assumption is that since religious assertions play a role in the life of believers, they therefore have a meaning. The philosophical enterprise is then to reveal what they mean and how they are related to the sentences of other language-games.

In this chapter and the following one we shall examine the work of some widely read thinkers who have either contributed to the analytic tradition on this subject or who have attempted to deal with the problem of religious language as it is posed within the framework of that tradition.

"Gods"

Renewed impetus for work in philosophical theology came in
1941 from John Wisdom's now-classical essay, "Gods." [1] It dealt
with the question of God's existence, and focused not on whether
there is a God or not but, in keeping with the temper of current
English philosophy, on the nature of the dispute between theist
and atheist. The problem of the meaning of religious language is
never mentioned explicitly, but the essay has had a profound influence on those for whom this issue is of central importance.
Later developments in this area appear in "Gods" in germinal
form. Subsequent writers constructed their own parables in imita-
tion of Wisdom's parable of the Invisible Gardener in order to illuminate one or another facet of religious belief and language:

> Once upon a time two explorers came upon a clearing
> in the jungle. In the clearing were growing many
> flowers and many weeds. One explorer says, "Some
> gardener must tend this plot." The other disagrees,
> "There is no gardener." So they pitch their tents and set
> a watch. No gardener is ever seen. "But perhaps he is an
> invisible gardener." So they set up a barbed-wire fence.
> They electrify it. They patrol it with bloodhounds. . . .
> But no shrieks ever suggest that some intruder has re-
> ceived a shock. No movements of the wire ever betray an
> invisible climber. The bloodhounds never give cry. "But
> there is a gardener, invisible, intangible, insensible to
> electric shocks, a gardener who has no scent and makes
> no sound, a gardener who comes secretly to look after
> the garden which he loves." At last the sceptic despairs,
> "But what remains of your original assertion? Just how
> does what you call an invisible, intangible, eternally
> elusive gardener differ from an imaginary gardener or
> even from no gardener at all?" [2]

---

[1] A recent reprinting is in Antony Flew, ed., *Logic and Language,* First and
Second Series (New York: Doubleday Anchor, 1965), pp. 194–214 (hereafter
cited as Wisdom, "Gods," in Flew, *Logic*).

[2] This is Flew's paraphrase of the parable, as given in Antony Flew and
Alasdair MacIntyre, eds., *New Essays in Philosophical Theology* (London:
SCM Press, 1955), p. 96 (hereafter cited as Flew, *New Essays*). For the original
parable, cf. Wisdom, "Gods," in Flew, *Logic,* pp. 200–201.

The existence of God, Wisdom maintains, is no longer an experimental issue in the way it once was. Theists still pray, of course, and believe that their prayers make a difference. But since we have a better idea of how nature works, the method of Elijah on Mount Carmel of deciding what God or gods exist is far less appropriate today than it was then. This does not mean, however, that the question of God's existence is not a factual one. But it does mean that there is something other than factual concerns involved in the dispute between theist and atheist, and this "other" is not merely verbal quibbling over whether or not, for example, we should call a given natural phenomenon "mind-like" and thereby imply the existence of a Cosmic Intelligence. The dispute is more like a legal one, in which the facts are agreed upon by all concerned, but disagreement still exists on how these facts ought to be interpreted; or even like the dispute over whether a work of art is beautiful or not. The issue of theism vs. atheism hinges then on the different ways of looking at evidence, or what connections and contrasts one finds in experience, and on what standpoints and attitudes one might adopt toward them.

There are many who believe that "something watches in the hills and manages the stars." [3] And there are many who find within themselves a mysterious power, stronger than the human. Artists and writers no less than scientists show us reality and bring us exhilaration and peace, releasing us from bondage into freedom. The many ways of salvation they show us are useful, despite the fact that they are always incomplete and apt to mislead. Not the worst of these, Wisdom concludes, is the way of salvation that speaks of man's oneness with God, and his with us.[4]

Wisdom thus finds religion's contribution to human life in the particular way of looking, seeing, appreciating, and evaluating experience that it offers to man. His claim that there is a factual core underlying these activities was centered upon by later thinkers who felt that the relationship between faith and facts required a closer look.

---

[3] Wisdom, "Gods," in Flew, *Logic*, p. 210.
[4] *Ibid.*, p. 214.

Positivists and Parable-Tellers

According to Antony Flew,[5] Wisdom's parable highlights the fundamental difficulty besetting religious discourse—its compatibility with every state of affairs. Language may assert something quite definite, only to retreat and retreat again in the face of opposing or nonconfirming evidence, the process ending only when what is stated is no longer capable of being verified or falsified, that is, when it has been removed from the realm of the meaningful. He writes: "Someone may dissipate his assertion completely without noticing that he has done so. A fine brash hypothesis may thus be killed by inches, the death by a thousand qualifications." [6] The peculiarity of religious language is that it is not open to any falsification whatever. Whenever a fact is served in evidence against a religious statement, the latter is qualified in order to save it. If, for example, we are told that God loves us like a father loves his children, this statement is qualified in some way—"God's love is not a merely human love" or is an "inscrutable love"—in the face of evidence which would seem to falsify it, the death of a child from inoperable cancer, for example. But

> what is this assurance of God's (appropriately qualified) love worth, what is this apparent guarantee really a guarantee against? Just what would have to happen not merely (morally and wrongly) to tempt us but also (logically and rightly) to entitle us to say "God does not love us" or even "God does not exist"? [7]

For Flew, theistic language is doomed, since its compatibility with every state of affairs forces it to be devoid of any factual content. To submit it to falsification in the interest of insuring its meaningfulness is to submit it to the possibility of disproof—a possibility that no theist will allow.

For somewhat different reasons, Bernard Williams agrees with

---

[5] Flew, *New Essays,* pp. 96 ff.

[6] *Ibid.,* p. 97.

[7] *Ibid.,* p. 99.

Flew's conclusions.[8] Theological language, as language about God, falls into a kind of inherent incomprehensibility, since it must postulate at some level links or relationships between a supernatural God and a natural world, for example, the Incarnation of God. The statement of these relationships will be unsatisfactory, however, since the concepts they employ (fatherhood, love) are acquired in a human context and are used to speak about the relations of humans to humans. To extrapolate these terms from the human context to speak of the human-divine relationship does not solve the problem; it merely poses it again. "For the extrapolation required is an extrapolation to infinity, and in even trying to give a sense to this we encounter the incomprehensibility." [9] Nor can this incomprehensibility be welcomed on the grounds that it leaves room for faith. It might be strange to be asked to have faith despite logical difficulties, but it is even stranger still to be asked to have faith in something that is not properly understood. Faith might be a way of believing something, as opposed to believing it on evidence; but it cannot be a way of stepping from what is understood to what is not understood. What, in fact, is the difference between believing something incomprehensible and disbelieving it? The only appropriate stand one may take when confronted with incomprehensibility is to demand clarification. Belief must wait upon the provision of a content to believe.[10]

Let us look at the following examples from parable-tellers:

> Once upon a time there was a lunatic who believed that all dons were plotting to murder him. His friends, concerned over his state of mind, introduced him to the mildest dons they could find. But to no avail; the lunatic was still convinced that all dons were plotting against his life, and accounted for their mild behavior towards him as part of their diabolical cunning.[11]

---

[8] Bernard Williams, "Tertullian's Paradox," in Flew, *New Essays,* pp. 187 ff.
[9] *Ibid.,* p. 204.
[10] *Ibid.,* pp. 209–211.
[11] This is a summary of Richard M. Hare's parable, as given in his contribution to Flew, *New Essays,* pp. 99 ff.

By means of this parable, Richard M. Hare introduces the concept of a *blik*. A *blik* is neither an assertion nor a system of assertions. It can perhaps be best described as an attitude or a framework for evaluation or explanation. The lunatic has an insane *blik* about dons, his friends a right one. We have *bliks* about other things as well. One such *blik* is the expectation that the properties of matter will remain constant; this allows us to drive confident that the steering in our cars will not behave erratically. We have others about things happening in the world for discoverable reasons, which allow us to explain, predict, and plan. A *blik* is not a meaningful assertion in Flew's sense of that term, since it is compatible with every state of affairs. But this is not to say that it is not important. There is a great difference between the lunatic's *blik* about dons and his friends', and there is a great difference between someone who believes that there are discoverable reasons for whatever happens and someone who believes that events occur by pure, unpredictable chance.

Religion, Hare argues, is a *blik*. The statements by which believers express their religious *blik,* such as "God exists" or "God loves us like a father loves his children," cannot be settled by reference to what happens in the world. To ask them to function as explanations, which is what Flew seems to want, is to mistake their status and render them ludicrous. While they may be compatible with every state of affairs, this does not mean that they are not important or make no great difference in the life of the person who might hold them.[12]

> Once upon a time, in a time of war in an occupied country, a member of the resistance meets a Stranger who impresses him deeply and who promises to help the resistance movement. He urges the partisan to have faith in him, no matter what. Later on, the Stranger is seen helping members of the resistance, and the partisan sees in this confirmation of his trust in the Stranger. At other times, the Stranger is seen handing over patriots to the occupying powers. But still the partisan's faith holds

[12] *Ibid.*, pp. 100–102.

strong. "The Stranger knows best," he says to his grum-
bling compatriots. "But what," they ask, "would the
Stranger have to do to make you admit that you are
wrong, and that the Stranger is not on our side?" But
the partisan refuses to answer: he will not put the
Stranger to the test.[13]

How long will the partisan be able to maintain his belief in the
Stranger? That depends on the nature of the impression the
Stranger makes on him, Basil Mitchell replies. He *does* admit that
the Stranger's behavior will have a bearing on his belief, and it is
only if he experiences the force of the conflict between his faith
and the Stranger's behavior that he can be regarded as sane and
reasonable in his belief.

The partisan's attitude to the Stranger is not a *blik,* for events
can count against it, while by Hare's accounting nothing can count
against a *blik.* The partisan has a reason for his faith in the
Stranger, whereas Hare's lunatic has no reason for his *blik* about
dons.

"The Stranger is on our side" is never allowed to be conclusively falsified by the partisan, and in this way it resembles the
statement "God loves men." To both of these statements three different approaches are possible: (1) they may be considered provi-
sional hypotheses which are to be discarded if experience tells
against them; (2) they are significant articles of faith; (3) they are
merely vacuous formulae to which experience can make no difference. Because of his faith, the Christian cannot adopt the first alternative. He may be tempted to adopt the third. But he does not
have to, and if he does, "it is a failure in faith as well as in
logic." [14]

> Two men are traveling together along a road. One be-
> lieves that it leads to the Celestial City. The pleasant
> stretches of road are interpreted by him as designed by
> the King of the City to encourage him along his way.

[13] This is a summary of Basil Mitchell's parable, as given in his contribution
to Flew, *New Essays,* pp. 103 ff.
[14] *Ibid.,* pp. 104–105.

> The hardships he sees as trials devised by the King to
> make him a worthy citizen of the City. The other trav-
> eler believes none of this. For him the journey is an
> aimless and unavoidable ramble. The road is there and
> must be traveled. There is only the luck of the road in
> good weather and bad.[15]

According to this parable as told by John Hick, theist and atheist inhabit the same world. They are distinguished from one another not in terms of what they might experience here and now,
but in what they expect when history is completed. The theist believes that history will have fulfilled the purpose of creating children of God. Death is not the end of all experience, but the beginning of a new kind of experience as man inhabits a spirit world in
a spirit body and apprehends the direct expression of the divine
purpose, while always conscious of existing in the presence of
God.

None of this may occur, of course. The atheist may be right;
there may be neither King nor City, only the luck of the road in
good weather and bad. But the expectation of experience is sufficient to mark a meaningful distinction between atheist and theist
and to insure that the statements of Christian belief are genuine,
that is, meaningful, assertions. Positivism objected to religious
language on the grounds that it said nothing about experience.
Hick counters that it does, even though the experience to which it
is relevant will begin only after life has ended.[16]

What do the parable tellers show about religious discourse?
Many would agree with the basic thrust of Hare's position that a
religious statement can be used to indicate an attitude or to provide a framework for the evaluation and explanation of experience.
It is common for a believer to interpret his experience within a
broad framework which he holds by faith. Many of his statements
about God—"God loves us all like a father loves his children"—are
not hypotheses, read from some state of affairs and framed to explain it as a scientific hypothesis is framed to explain phenomena.

---

[15] This is a summation of John Hick's parable from his *Faith and Knowledge*
(Ithaca, N.Y.: Cornell University Press, 1957), pp. 150–151.

[16] *Ibid.*, pp. 152, 155, 162.

Rather, they express a point of view, an angle of interpretation, a way in which experience is understood. The believer does not go to experience and draw his faith; he finds his interpretive categories in faith and then goes to experience with them. But a process as sophisticated as this can often be runs the risk of being misunderstood. A statement may appear to be a straightforward description—"God loves men" may appear to describe God in the same way that "Smith loves his wife" describes Smith—when close attention to its usage may reveal that it is not assimilable to a descriptive statement at all, but is instead an interpretive statement. When a religious assertion is used to indicate an attitude or provide a way of understanding experience, it is consequently more illuminating to see it against the background of Hare's *blik* than in terms of a simple descriptive statement that one might find in a scientific textbook.

But, as Flew reminds us, Hare's account of religious language is incomplete, if only because it implies that as *bliks,* religious statements can be neither true or false.[17] Most believers would wish to resist that consequence. They would readily admit that religious language often has an interpretive role to play, but unless a framework of interpretation can be independently justified—unless, that is, one can claim on its behalf that it is, in some sense of that term, *true*—it is surely arbitrary and specious. Believers are confident that their interpretation of experience in the light of God's loving care is not weak-minded delusion, because there is good reason, they claim, to hold that there *is* a God who loves man. But this does not solve the problem of religious discourse; rather, it poses the problem in one of its more difficult forms. If it is a fact that God loves men, it is not a fact in the sense that the sun is shining now is a fact, or that it is a fact that Jones loves his son, or even in the sense that evolution may be spoken of as a fact. All of these would fall in the face of opposed empirical evidence. But the "religious fact" refuses to permit such evidence to count decisively against it.

All this means is that there are facts and facts, and we might

---

[17] Flew, *New Essays,* pp. 107–108.

have different ways of coming to know different kinds of facts. We might know it is raining because we can look out of the window and see it; that Jones loves his son because, despite some evidence to the contrary, there is a tremendous amount of evidence in favor of this supposition; that evolution occurred because we have no other way that accounts as successfully for existing biological data. We might know, too, that God loves men because we have been told so by someone who knows this and because we have trust and faith in that claim.

It is here that the role of commitment that underlies so much of religious language begins to be significant for a more complete account of this matter. In Mitchell's parable, the partisan's trust in the Stranger is not blind, since it is rooted in the depth of the impression that the Stranger made on him. Nor is this trust a *blik*, since the partisan can cite reasons, *good* reasons, for his trust, and because the Stranger's subsequent behavior has a bearing on his belief. Analogously, the religious man's faith and the sentences which express it depend, at least in part, on the impression made on him by the object of his faith—God. Mitchell will not compromise the claim that at least some religious statements are *bona fide* assertions, although he seems to recognize that their logic is different from that of more ordinary assertions. They are not tentative hypotheses to be rejected if experience tells against them, but are "significant articles of faith." But how a significant article of faith might be related to other statement-functions or to evidence that mitigates against it, and how all this might answer the positivist indictment of religious discourse, Mitchell does not specify.

Hick's approach to the issue is straightforward. He seems to accept the positivist understanding of meaning at face value, but argues that Christian religious discourse measures up to that conception since it refers to an experience that will occur after death. Unfortunately, however, this runs into serious difficulties. One may well wonder what an experience may be like that occurs in a nonspatial world to men who have nonspatial bodies. While the word *experience* has many meanings, to speak of post-mortem experience in Hick's manner seems to extend the meaning of the term to such a degree that it hardly says anything any longer. But even if the word-extension problem can be satisfactorily resolved, Hick's position still fails to meet one element of the positivist problem, namely, how one might discover here and now what a religious statement means. As Flew asks, what is one saying when one says "God is good"? What is the guarantee of God's goodness a guarantee against? Hick's position gives no basis for answering. To say that "God is good" will be understood only when life ends is of little help to the person who might refuse to accept it until he knows what it means, or who, to use Bernard Williams' language, suspends belief until its content is specified.[18]

The Essence of Religious Language

We noted earlier that the "emotive" category which positivism had erected as a catchall for important but nonsignificant statements soon proved unsatisfactory, since it hid important differences in statement-functions under a single emotion-charged label. It was an especially clumsy way of dealing with religious statements which perform a great variety of tasks in the lives of believers. The result was that philosophers considered it advisable to chart the specific functions these might serve. If this marked an advance over positivism, it was a small one, since these investigations were premised on the assumption that, important though they might be, the statements involved were nonetheless cognitively valueless.

An early and extensively read work was Richard B. Braithwaite's *An Empiricist's View of the Nature of Religious Belief*.[19] There are, on the surface at least, many different kinds of religious statements. But Braithwaite found them all to contain a pri-

---

[18] For further discussion of Hick's "eschatological verification," see Kai Nielsen, "Eschatological Verification," *Canadian Journal of Theology*, IX (1963), pp. 271–281; George I. Mavrodes, "God and Verification," *Ibid.*, X (1964), pp. 187–191; and Kai Nielsen, "God and Verification Again," *Ibid.*, XI (1965), pp. 135–141.

[19] Richard B. Braithwaite, *An Empiricist's View of the Nature of Religious Belief* (Cambridge: Cambridge University Press, 1955).

mary element: they are all used as moral assertions. Ethical language thus provides the best model by means of which they can be appreciated. Such language does not record our emotional response to an action as positivism had said it did, but registers our intention to act in a certain way under given circumstances. Certain religious statements, Braithwaite found, indicate our willingness to behave in an other-centered or "agapeistic" manner, which not only means that we act charitably and with our actions designed to foster the good of others, but requires that we cultivate the inner feelings and emotional attitudes appropriate to such behavior.[20]

The work of T.R. Miles,[21] though essentially following Braithwaite's angle of interpretation, is broader in scope and more detailed and articulate in its presentation. Miles distinguishes three ways in which talk about God can be classified: as "simple literal theism," "qualified literal theism," and "the language of parable." Simple literal theism is that way of speaking of God or the gods in which their presence and activity are held to be directly observable, as, for example, the poets' descriptions of the involvement of Greek gods in human affairs. This kind of language is open to straightforward verification and is therefore meaningful; but it is also false. Since, however, Christians do not generally speak of God in this manner, simple literal theism may be ignored. Qualified literal theism speaks of God as intervening in human affairs, except that, unlike the anthropomorphic deities of Greece, he is neither visible nor tangible. Statements of this kind ("God intervened at Dunkirk") pretend to give factual information. But Miles believes that there are good reasons for describing as factually significant *only* those statements whose usage is governable by empirical criteria,[22] and as no such criteria can be provided by means of which we could decide whether or not an event was due to God's

<hr/>

[20] *Ibid.*, p. 19.
[21] T. R. Miles, *Religion and the Scientific Outlook* (New York: Humanities Press, 1959) (hereafter cited as Miles, *Religion*). But cf. his "On Excluding the Supernatural," *Religious Studies*, I (1965), p. 150 for a later modification of this early position.
[22] Miles, *Religion*, pp. 43–46, 141.

intervening activity, it would be as pointless to assert his involvement in it as it would be to deny it. The language of qualified literal theism is meaningless.[23]

The indefensibility of the above two ways of speaking of God forces Miles to take "the way of silence." This is not to be taken to mean that all talk of God must come to an end. The believer can still tell "theistic parables," thereby distinguishing himself from the unbeliever. A parable, in general, has three characteristics: (1) the question of its literal truth or falsity is not important; (2) it contains, for the most part, empirical assertions; and (3) it conveys a message. These three characteristics are found in the language of Christian faith, and for purposes of illustration Miles selects the opening words of Genesis, "In the beginning God created the heaven and the earth."

(1) It makes no difference whether this account of creation is literally true or not. By use of a quasi-historical story, timeless truths are brought dramatically to our attention, and these truths are what the account is all about. (2) Within the context of parable-talk, the Genesis account contains statements that are empirically verifiable. The words involved are linked with our familiar experience; we know what it would be like for a powerful and loving craftsman to create something, and we can imagine what it would be like for a new object to occupy empty space. (3) Finally, the story of creation, provided we take it seriously, places on us the obligation of looking at the world in a new way. The truth it conveys, its cash value so to speak, lies in the fact that it leads to the recognition that everything is part of the divine purpose, and that God is to be seen not only in a cosmic event or the beauties of nature, but even in trivial, routine happenings. Religious beliefs are tied to one another, and the doctrine of creation is connected with others that speak of the incarnation and atonement. Together with the parable of an all-wise, all-good father, these doctrines lead to the important moral conclusion that one's highest duty is to do God's will.[24]

---

[23] *Ibid.*, pp. 145–149.
[24] *Ibid.*, p. 169.

Why do we accept one parable rather than another? In the last resort the answer lies more with personal conviction than rational argument. But this is not to say that reasons cannot be given for accepting one parable and rejecting another, even though it must be realized that these reasons cannot be expected to settle matters conclusively. We might choose to accept or reject a parable because of its *relationship to empirical fact*. The existence of evil may cause someone to reject the parable of an infinitely perfect father, or if it could be demonstrated that there is no free choice, it might be inappropriate to accept the parable of Adam and Eve and a primeval choice of evil. Again, we might choose one parable rather than another because of its *connection with moral beliefs*. The acceptance of a particular parable (God as a loving father) may commit us to moral positions of which we approve highly (an altruistic ethic), or conversely, if we have independent reasons for holding a moral belief, we might be attracted to a parable because of its connection with that belief.[25]

It is somewhat difficult to make any clear-cut distinction between the language of parable and that of qualified literal theism, because there are many ambiguous cases in which, from the context, we are not sure what kind of language someone is using. One needs to develop a feel for both sorts of language in order to distinguish some of the more difficult cases. There are, however, two general, though not always reliable, pointers to help us distinguish between them. First, the language of parable is somewhat removed from our everyday language, whereas that of qualified literal theism is not. "In the beginning God created the heaven and the earth" is not the language we use in ordinary life; "God made the world" is, and would lend itself rather easily to a literal interpretation. Second, the language of parable speaks of God in ways that we would never use to speak of ordinary people. We would never think of saying of someone that "he is love," and this leads us to suspect that "God is love" is parable language.[26]

Of what sort is the dispute between people who hold different

25 *Ibid.*, pp. 170–173.
26 *Ibid.*, pp. 173–175.

parables, and what is involved when a person changes from one set of parables to another? All people, theist and atheist alike, hold to parables. "All living involves the implicit acceptance of one parable or another," [27] and "the question is not whether to tell parables, but what parable to tell." [28] Theist and atheist differ not in the facts they have at their disposal (which, according to verificationist techniques, must be the same for both), but in how they see those facts, in the parables they tell about them. Disagreement over parable choice is therefore not a factual disagreement, but is like a disagreement over the choice of a set of moral values. Even though reasons for one's choice may be offered, the moral values one accepts, like the parables one tells, cannot be decided by reference to technical advisers, but are ultimately a matter for personal choice. This does not devalue the importance of the parable chosen, since it would have cash value in our actions and commitments. To speak of God as a loving father to all men leads to the adoption of altruistic attitudes and commitments which are manifested by our behavior; to hold the parable that life is senseless and that we live only briefly and are then forever extinguished may lead to selfish attitudes and actions.[29] The change from one set of parables to another requires a "change of heart" or "conversion," whose meaning is found, and genuineness judged, in the actions that accompany it.[30]

Many writers have disagreed with the Braithwaite-Miles belief that ethical language provides the best understanding of religious discourse. Kai Nielsen suggested that it would be more completely illuminated in terms of the *ideological sentence*. An ideological sentence appears to be an empirical hypothesis, but is really a

---

[27] *Ibid.*, pp. 178–179.

[28] *Ibid.*, p. 179.

[29] It is arguable whether Miles can ultimately defend his distinction between believer and unbeliever. If the only cash value of a parable lies in the attitudes, etc. to which it gives rise, it is easily imaginable that believer and unbeliever might have these in common, though one backs them with a theistic parable and the other with a nontheistic one. A life of altruistic service, for example, is hardly the exclusive property of those who tell theistic parables.

[30] Miles, *Religion*, pp. 177–178.

value judgment whose function is to recommend actions and attitudes. Statements about God seem simultaneously to indicate how we behave or intend to behave, to evaluate our experience, and to express and evoke commitments—all this while masquerading as an empirical hypothesis.[31] It is their deceptive grammatical form that leads believers to think that they are making straightforward factual judgments. But as ideological sentences they function by affecting our awareness of what the world is like: they give rise to attitudes and behavior patterns, and soothe our anxieties through reference to God's fatherly care. Beyond this Nielsen can find no content in religious assertions; all cognitive claims made on their behalf are so much "sound and fury" that denote next to nothing, although they express the deepest and most valuable of human concerns.[32]

The psychological importance of religious belief is similarly identified by Curt J. Ducasse, who defines religion as "any set of beliefs—together with the observances, feelings, and injunctions based on them—which, insofar as dominantly believed by a person, tend to perform for him personally, and for society through him, certain highly important functions." [33] While a religious belief is essentially a tool useful in the performance of important social and personal functions, it does not present itself in this way but claims, instead, to be objectively true. Ducasse interprets this in such a way that Christian beliefs are put on the same logical footing as myths; neither myth nor article of faith has to be logical, clear, mutually consistent, or objectively true in order to perform its vital psychological functions.[34]

In general, a subject may be approached on a subjective or an objective level, according to Gordon Kaufman,[35] and it is a

---

[31] Kai Nielsen, "On Talk About God," *The Journal of Philosophy*, LV (1958), p. 889.

[32] *Ibid.*, pp. 889–890. See also his "On Speaking of God," *Theoria*, XXVIII (1962), p. 137. This contains a more explicit presentation of his earlier position.

[33] Curt J. Ducasse, "Christianity, Rationality, and Faith," *The Review of Religion*, XXII (1958), p. 134.

[34] *Ibid.*, p. 136.

[35] Gordon Kaufman, "Philosophy of Religion: Subjective or Objective?" *The Journal of Philosophy*, LV (1958), pp. 57–70.

subjective approach that reveals the value and meaning of religious statements. Religious terms, symbols, and rituals are all expressive of certain definite realities met subjectively in human existence. Unless we are aware of these realities, we lose the point of such religious expressions. This does not mean, however, that a philosophical approach to religion will necessarily degenerate into a personal confession. Rather, it is possible to develop a view of the nature and structure of human existence in which the demands of personal subjectivity can be shown to have validity for all men. Within this subjectivity, highly personal yet sharing points of contact with the subjectivity of others, we can find that religion is conceivable as a source of "the answer to or resolution of the problems and tensions which lie deep within man's subjectivity," [36] the problem of being free while being controlled by forces that tend to decrease our freedom, for example. The statements of religion, along with religious practices and symbols, are all symbolic ways of stating or answering these problems.[37]

While the preceding writers have isolated the psychological value of religious beliefs and statements as their essential component, Abraham Cronbach [38] considers religious language to be essentially evaluative of experience. It is quite easy, he writes, to point out the flaws in the cognitive claims which religious statements make. But religion consists not only in what it alleges, but also in what it manifests, and if we judge it in terms of this latter, our appraisal of it may be more sympathetic. One may well deny any factual content to the story of the cleavage of the Red Sea yet regard with sympathy the cravings which the legend satisfies. What religious language does is help us evaluate our experience. So conceived, God becomes "superbly real" as a means of dramatizing

---

[36] *Ibid.*, p. 66.

[37] Thus: "As long as I cannot find in the interconnected system of meanings which structures my subjectivity the relationships which can enable me to understand why it is that someone might say 'Atman is Brahman,' I have not understood just what subjective meanings these terms express, which is to say, I have not yet understood these terms." *Ibid.*, p. 61.

[38] Abraham Cronbach, "The Linguistics of Theism," *The Hibbert Journal*, LII (1953–1954), pp. 9–16.

experience, whereas as an alleged entity he might seem incredible.[39] The same point is put another way by William E. Kennick, who finds that religious statements, like all other statements, are to be judged in terms of their use.[40] Since the use of a statement is known through its effects, to find out if religious language has meaning we must look at the effects it has. Its goal, he continues, "is the evocation or sustenance of some attitude which is deemed of utmost importance," that is, the religious attitude.[41] An attitude is religious

> if it assumes a vital, and above all *pervasive* role in the
> life of a man or of a society, conditioning, determining,
> and focusing all or most other attitudes and reactions—
> those which have as their objects the natural world, cul-
> tural institutions, and other men and other societies, and
> even, or perhaps especially, those attitudes which a man
> takes towards himself. . . .[42]

Religion is not, therefore, a matter of cognitive claims, even though these have played an historical part in religion; the purpose of religious language is to "articulate, arouse, sustain and modify attitudes." [43]

We might close this section by mentioning Thomas McPherson, who agrees that the verification principle has eliminated religious language but considers that this might be all to the good for religion itself.[44] "The things that theologians try to say (or some of them) belong to the class of things that just cannot be said," [45] he writes. But this will not greatly discourage the theist who cares more for worship than for words, and it might even be construed as helping the truly religious person who has been tempted to seek God in the wrong places. Thus

---

[39] *Ibid.,* p. 15.

[40] William E. Kennick, "The Language of Religion," *The Philosophical Review,* LXV (1956), pp. 56–71.

[41] *Ibid.,* p. 68.

[42] *Ibid.*

[43] *Ibid.,* p. 66.

[44] Thomas McPherson, "Religion as the Inexpressible," in Flew, *New Essays,* pp. 131–143.

[45] *Ibid.,* p. 133.

a branding of religious assertions as "nonsense" need not be anti-religious. It can be interpreted as an attack on those who in the name of religion are perverting religion. It can be interpreted as a return to the truth about religion. Otto[46] conceived himself . . . to be recovering the essential element in religion—which had been in danger of being lost under a cloud of rationalizing. What is essential about religion is its nonrational side, the part that cannot be . . . put into words.[47]

Positivism is the enemy of the theologian who tries to say the unsayable; but it is the friend of the religious man who is willing to leave the unsayable unsaid.

"The Intention of Those Who Speak"

When St. Thomas Aquinas dealt with the problem of the logic of theological statements, he examined the position that held them to mean in a negative way.[48] So, for example, those who hold this view would make "God is good" equivalent to "God is not bad," or "God is just" equivalent to "God is not unjust." Aquinas cited three reasons why he found this view unacceptable; the third of these is particularly relevant for us who would attempt to evaluate the views of religious discourse presented in the above section. The negative-meaning theory, Aquinas wrote, is inadequate because "this is against the intention of those who speak of God." [49] The person who says "God is good" means something more than "God is not bad"; and, we might add, it can be taken as a general guideline that an adequate account of how theological or religious statements mean must carefully respect the intention of those who use those statements. We do not need a philosopher to teach us

---

[46] Rudolf Otto (1869–1937), German theologian, author of *The Idea of the Holy, Naturalism and Religion, The Philosophy of Religion.*

[47] *Ibid.,* p. 139.

[48] *Summa Theologiae,* I, 13, 2.

[49] *Ibid., corpus.* This entire question is highly illuminative of this issue, not only as it is posed by Aquinas himself, but as it is discussed in the analytic tradition as well. See also the parallel discussion in the *Summa Contra Gentiles,* I, 30–36.

how to speak; one may help us, however, toward a deeper appreciation of what we have to say.

This does not mean, however, that we must close the door on the critical enterprise. In his evaluation of religion, for example, the philosopher may find that the logic of some particular bit of discourse is muddled—as in the case of those who suggest that the biblical account of creation is on the same logical footing as an astronomer's theory of cosmic formation—or that it fails to achieve the purpose intended by its author. Or it may be found that the rules governing some item of religious language are self-contradictory or incompatible with the rules governing the use of some other item. It would then be the task of the philosopher to exhibit such paradoxical and untenable situations. But a critical job along these lines can and should be carried out in an atmosphere of understanding and respect. It is philosophically odious to lay down *a priori* rules dictating how a given language-game ought to be conducted. The philosopher has the more patient, if somewhat less dramatic, task of describing actual language-practices, illuminating their contours, and exhibiting their rules and relationships with "the intention of those who speak" as point of departure and standard of judgment. If, in the course of this activity, he is led to judge that a particular language-game fails to be clear or consistent, his judgment can be tempered with appreciation of the ends which such uses were designed to serve.

The writers surveyed above, and many others whose work proceed along similar lines, have attempted to display the fundamental character of religious language. But their accounts, for all their illuminative value, appear so grossly oversimplified that, while one may be thankful for what they reveal, one still remains appalled at what yet remains to be said. One does not have to listen long in order to realize that religious language expresses attitudes, focuses and gives direction to our many commitments, provides a framework for interpretation and explanation of experience, states and resolves problems of an existential sort, or has various psychological and social functions to perform. But it is simply false to say that any or all of these are involved in every religious use of language; a little investigation will turn up instances which cannot, without massive forcing, be subsumed under these categories. Such reductionism fails, in the end, to respect the intention of believers.

We can see this from another angle. Much postpositivist work in religion has been dominated by the assumption that there is a single, essential element underlying the surface complexity of religious discourse. Why is this assumption made? Probably because a number of different statement-functions are given the same name ("religious"), and this leads some to assume that they all *must* possess some single feature which the common name designates. Despite the fact that eminent philosophers have, from time to time, come to think that different objects or activities which are called by a common name must share a common feature (one may recall Plato's search for the supposed essence of piety to which the name "piety" corresponds),[50] this seems to be an illustration of Bacon's idol of the marketplace, or an instance of failure to heed Wittgenstein's warning that the human mind runs the danger of being bewitched by language. When this assumption is made, however, another factor comes into play. Elements of many language-games play roles in religious discourse, and the discovery of any one of these—commitment-expression, attitude-formation, or whatever —then leads the thinker to believe that he has found *the* one essential element which, because they are all called by the common name, religious sentences must contain. But it is soon realized that full justice has not been done to a complex subject, and another interpretation, often equally as reductionist as the one it attempts to replace, is then presented.

But if the above positions fail to be complete in scope, they are further flawed by the usual assumption of their proponents that religious statements cannot be true since they are literally meaningless. A believer may well allow that when he speaks of God's loving care, for example, he is indicating that he has opted for an

---

[50] Plato, *Euthyphro*, 5: "Is not piety in every action always the same? and impiety, again—is it not always the opposite of piety, and also the same with itself, having, as impiety, one notion which includes whatever is impious?" Cf. *Republic*, X, 596. This quotation is taken from Benjamin Jowett, trans., *The Dialogues of Plato*, 2 vols. (New York: Random House, 1937).

altruistic ethic, or that he sees the events of his life in the light of his faith in divine concern, or that he finds in his belief the resolution of important dilemmas he meets in his life. For he means all this, *and more*. The ethical, attitudinal, and psychological ramifications of his belief are not symptoms of weak-mindedness, delusion, or neurosis, he insists, simply because it is true, *objectively* true, that God loves men. But since the above authors consider openness to empirical falsification and verification a necessary condition for calling any nontautological assertion true, they are not prepared to seek a fair understanding of what the word *true* might mean when spoken of to refer to statements about God. Once again, the intention of those who speak has not been respected.

Nor, we may add, does it seem particularly promising to look for religion's life in the death of theology. There is worship as well as words, heart as well as head; and theologians realize that the Holy remains so far beyond human thought and speech that any pretense to enclose It in finite categories—"put [It] into words" —is impossible, if not blasphemous. But worship severed from rational reflection, articulation, purification, and restraint—all parts of the theological enterprise—comes perilously close to superstition and unwelcome irrationality. To surrender all claims to know the Holy fails to do justice to Christianity's paradoxical and profound insistence that it knows the unknown God.

In the following chapter we shall examine the work of some writers who have attempted, and are attempting, to make up these serious deficiencies. We shall examine efforts to chart the wide variety of religious discourse and to discuss its syntax. We shall also sketch, on the basis of what we have found, the sense in which at least some religious statements may be called "true."

IV

The Functions of
Religious Statements

Indeed, this is the situation, for, while we know of God what He
is not, what He is *remains quite unknown.*
                    St. Thomas Aquinas, *Summa Contra Gentiles,* III, 49.9.

*Our mistake is to look for an explanation when we ought to look
at what happens as a "proto-phenomenon". That is, where we
ought to have said:* this language-game is played.

*The question is not one of explaining a language-game by means
of our experience, but of noting a language-game.*
                    Ludwig Wittgenstein, *Philosophical Investigations* I, 654–655.

Introduction

   As we have seen, many of the early analytic philosophers of religion tended to reduce all religious discourse to some single type
or function, thus failing to respect the intention of those who
speak in religious ways. As "meaning," "literal meaning" and "empirical meaning" were taken equivalently, with the true/false categories belonging to meaningful statements alone, there could be no
satisfactory accounting for the believer's insistence that the statements he used to speak of God, man, and their relationship were
true. In recent years, however, writers have begun to rectify matters by, on the one hand, cataloging the many purposes religious
language may serve and relating them to their basis in faith, and
on the other, attempting to provide for an understanding of the
word *true* as it is applicable to religious discourse. In this chapter
we will examine some prominent instances of recent work bearing
on these topics.

The Functions of Religious Language

How does "The ways of the almighty and all-wise God are righteous, though beyond our understanding" function? [1] If it is taken by itself, one might expect that it is designed to provide some information about God's ways to man or about the limits of human understanding. While there may be uses in which either of these would be its primary intent, Robert Coburn chooses to explore its characteristics when it is designed primarily to answer a "religiously limiting question" such as "But why was *my* child crippled by polio?" In general, a limiting question is not one which, appearances aside, asks for and is answered by a response of either a practical or theoretical kind. Instead, it indicates that the questioner is in a spiritual condition of some kind, such as grief or despair. For example, if someone were to ask, "Why ought I to do what is right?" he need not be asking about the prudence of being moral. The very raising of the question may be an essential feature of a spiritual state or activity, such as a state of moral conflict in which moral demands are at odds with nonmoral interests or desires. Since it functions in this way, no answer of the kind one would give to an ordinary practical or theoretical question will do.[2] Religiously limiting statements answer religiously limiting questions in a variety of ways, and one of these is by means of a statement that is "logically complete." A logically complete statement is one whose acceptance makes it "logically odd" to ask the question which evoked it over again. Hence, if "But why was *my* child crippled by polio?" is not a straightforward practical or theoretical question (which might be answered, for example, by saying, "You forgot to have him vaccinated"), but is a religiously limiting question, the acceptance of the statement "The ways of the almighty and all-wise God are righteous, though beyond our understanding" would make it logically odd to ask the question

---

[1] Robert C. Coburn, "A Neglected Use of Theological Language," *Mind,* LXXII (1963), pp. 369–385.

[2] *Ibid.,* pp. 371, 373. A religiously limiting question has to do with problems of morale or questions of morals and the meaning of life. *Ibid.,* pp. 373–374.

again. If the question were to be asked again, it would indicate that one had either not understood or had not really accepted the given answer.[3]

It is surprising and unfortunate that the kind of exploration which Coburn's study exemplifies is a rarity in analytic literature.[4] It is surprising, since this is the kind of work one would have expected in large quantity in the wake of Wittgenstein's later view of meaning, with its emphasis on piecemeal charting of the parts of individual language-games. Undoubtedly, some of the interest in the hunt was lost when thinkers realized that their quarry—the essence of religious discourse—could not be captured in a ten-page article. It is unfortunate, since Coburn's analysis is free from the objectionable assumptions that vitiated earlier approaches and marks a significant advance over them in at least three ways. First, the statement is not considered apart from some concrete situation in which it could be actually used. Second, it is recognized, at least implicitly, that there are other situations in which the statement might be used and for which this account would not be satisfactory. Third, there is no suggestion that all religious statements function, or can function, in this way. Claims for the validity of the analysis extend no further than to other like statements similarly used. While this does not mean that it is impossible to give some general account of religious language in general, it does mean that any such account must be grounded in the close scrutiny of religious statements as they are actually used.

However, real progress in the area of religious language is continually made as writers attempt to identify the broad categories used to classify religious statements. Some of these categories are:

(1) *Historical.* Christian believers hold, as a matter of historical record, that certain events took place in connection with the birth,

---

[3] *Ibid.,* p. 376.

[4] For further examples of this kind of work, see Alastair McKinnon, "Unfalsifiability and Religious Belief," *Canadian Journal of Theology,* XII (1966), pp. 118–125, which analyzes possible uses of "God is Love," and his "The Meaning of Religious Assertions," *Encounter,* XXI (1960), pp. 398–407, which similarly investigates "Christ is Divine."

life, and death of Christ. These historical assertions, such as "Jesus was condemned to death by Pontius Pilate," are, it is claimed, not subject to criticism by verificationist techniques.

(2) *Definitional.* Though they might appear otherwise, some statements, such as "God is omnipotent," are really definitions. Only if a being were omnipotent would the Christian call him "God," from which it follows that to say "God is omnipotent" is, at least in some of its uses, to explicate one's understanding of the term *God* rather than to describe the divine nature.

(3) *Emotive.* Positivism drew attention to this function of religious statements, but mistakenly held that all religious assertions belong to this category. Some religious assertions, however, such as "I feel at peace with God," are used to describe the feelings and sentiments of the believer.

(4) *Prescriptive.* Some religious statements assert policies of action or behavior which the believer follows or ought to follow: "If a man hits your right cheek, turn the other one to him as well." (Matthew 5:39–40).[5]

(5) *Invocative.* Such language is most often associated with prayer, when the individual is not speaking *about* God but *to* Him and desires to avail himself of his God-relationship: "O God, you know we are your people. . . ."

(6) *Accusatory.* These serve to call the individual's attention to his sinful state and need for salvation: ". . . all men from Jews to Greeks are under the condemnation of sin" (Romans 3:9).

(7) *Recollective.* Statements in this category function by reminding the believer that he owes his first allegiance to God and must seek the means to maintain it: "Set your heart on his kingdom and his goodness, and all these things will come to you as a matter of course" (Matthew 6:33).

(8) *Persuasive.* These are used to develop and foster the religious attitude in another: "No one approaches the Father except through me" (John 14:6).

(9) *Invitational.* These serve to invite the individual to enter

---

[5] All references to the New Testament are drawn from *The New Testament in Modern English,* trans. J. B. Phillips (London: Geoffrey Bles, 1960).

into a God-relationship: ". . . I did not come to invite the 'righteous' but the 'sinners' " (Matthew 9:13).

(10) *Descriptive*. These are used to speak of God's nature and his ways to man: "God loves all men as his children." [6]

It is obvious that these categories are not exhaustive; a little reflection will turn up further functions which religious statements serve. Nor do the statements given to illustrate the various categories belong exclusively to any one of them. One can imagine a context in which the statement "With God anything is possible" (Matthew 19:26) is used *descriptively*, by a missionary speaking of the Christian God to a group of nonbelievers, for example, as well a context in which it is used to *reassure* and *remind* someone of the power of prayer. We can imagine contexts, even, in which a religious statement is used to serve simultaneously a variety of ends.

Now while there are resemblances between religious and nonreligious uses of language (religiously invitational statements being, for instance, similar in many ways to ordinary invitations), this must not be allowed to obscure their fundamental differences. For instance, "Jones loves Smith," an ordinary descriptive statement, operates in situations whose characteristics are empirically identifiable—Jones makes some extraordinary sacrifice on Smith's behalf—the words involved being used in straightforward, nonproblematic ways. But it is not immediately obvious in what situations a religiously descriptive statement like "God loves Smith" functions. Nor is it a simple matter to account for the fact that the words involved, though they often appear in ordinary discourse, are used in extraordinary ways. Is there any feature, or group of features, that would serve to characterize the *situations* in which religiously descriptive sentences, and religious assertions in general, may be employed? And how account for the odd syntactical

---

[6] Discussion of some of these examples may be found in Mary C. Rose, "The Language of Religion," *Anglican Theological Review*, XL (1958), pp. 108–119; Alexander Gibson, "Empirical Evidence and Christian Faith," *The Journal of Religion*, XXXVI (1956), pp. 24–35; and Luther Binkley, "What Characterizes Religious Language?" *Journal for the Scientific Study of Religion*, II (1962), pp. 18–22.

properties which the words that compose these assertions often have?

The Syntax of Religious Language: Ian Ramsey

A religious situation, Ian Ramsey suggests, is characterized by a *discernment* that is fuller and more complete than the ordinary perceptual discernment which we may have, and to which a person responds by a total *commitment*.[7] Religious discernment sees a "depth" in a situation that is more than the sum total of the perceived facts. Imagine, Ramsey suggests, the setting of an English High Court: its participants in ceremonial robes and the situation marked by an impersonality exemplified by the fact that those involved have shed their names and are "the accused," "the prosecution," "the Chief Justice," and "the witness for the defense." One day the Chief Justice enters the court only to discover that the accused is his closest friend from undergraduate days. Here the impersonal situation "comes alive," is more than "what's seen," and takes on depth. This depth, the changed appreciation of the situation in which personal elements and interests are brought into play, may be reflected in the use of intrapersonal language that stands in marked contrast to the formal language of usual court proceedings.

Depth-discernment is not, of course, uniquely religious; it becomes so when it seeks to evoke a distinctive kind of commitment. This is the *religious* commitment, and it seems to have two characteristics: *breadth,* in that it is a commitment suited to the whole business of living and is not adopted in the interests of doing a certain job which will be changed when another comes along; and *depth,* in that it is life-dominating, central, and personally engaging as it gathers together and structures all the believer's diverse relationships, feelings, and attitudes.[8] In particular, the Christian's act of faith focuses on a "cosmic commitment" to Jesus, "the

---

[7] Ian T. Ramsey, *Religious Language: An Empirical Placing of Theological Phrases* (New York: The Macmillan Company, 1963), pp. 20–34 (hereafter cited as Ramsey, *Religious Language*).

[8] *Ibid.,* p. 39.

Christ who is organic to the old Israel and to the new Israel of his Church and through them to the whole of history." [9] Since religious belief thus finds its empirical basis in the religious discernment-commitment situation, it is to be expected that the *language* of belief will be logically odd in at least two ways: it will be "object language," so qualified that it becomes logically peculiar; and it will contain significant tautologies.

(1) *Religious language is object language, suitably qualified.*[10] Religious language speaks, as we have seen, about perceptual situations which differ in the depth they possess. Religious language is thus rooted in the language used in ordinary perceptual situations (object language), but must be appropriately qualified to encompass the difference that religious depth-discernment involves. We will see later on how this qualification is effected. Ramsey notes, with obvious reference to those critics who complain that religious language cannot be fully explicated in ordinary perceptual language, that if the religious commitment has a basis in a perceptual situation but goes beyond it, we ought not to expect that it can be fully "unpacked" in the language of perceptual constants alone.

(2) *Religious language contains significant tautologies.*[11] There are language-games in which tautologies function by commending key words or by indicating final options. Should a moralist be asked, "Why should I do my duty?" and respond, "Duty for duty's sake," he is commending the word *duty* as a key term for human life. His statement is a significant tautology, indicating that an irreducible posit has been attained—in this case, the ultimate moral commitment of that ethical system.

Significant tautologies are often used in religious discourse. One such instance is the expression "God is Love," which seems to have the following logical structure: by various accounts of human devotion, a religious situation may be evoked in which the person to whom the stories are told is led not only to admire goodness

---

[9] *Ibid.*, p. 41.
[10] *Ibid.*, p. 42.
[11] *Ibid.*, pp. 44 ff.

and love, but to respond to them by a total personal commitment. It is in relation to this that the religious man finds use for the terms *God* and *love*. His tautology "God is Love" is claiming that the word *God* can be used in relation to total commitment, approached through the partial commitments we usually describe by the word *love*. *God* is thus a key word, an irreducible posit, an ultimate in religious explanation which expresses the believer's commitment.

There are three kinds of expressions that frequently turn up in religious and theological discourse. They are (1) the terms of negative theology (*immutable, impassible*); (2) the positive terms by which God is characterized (*unity, perfection*); and (3) other traditional characterizations (*first cause, infinitely wise, infinitely good*). How do these differ from one another?

(1) *The terms of negative theology* have a twofold function.[12] They serve first to evoke the odd discernment that characterizes religious situations and which, once evoked, may lead to religious commitment. The terms *immutable* and *impassible* thus point to the mutable and passible features of ordinary experience. By negation they attempt to evoke the discernment of the changeless within change, or to ask the believer to look beyond all passible stories, especially when they deal with accounts of human relationships and treat them as inadequate. But second, these terms also serve notice that the word *God* holds a position outside the language of the mutable and the passible; such language is inadequate when speaking about him. Negative language thus emphasizes the fact that the language of ordinary perceptual situations is inadequate when speaking about God. In the end, negative language tells us next to nothing about him.[13]

(2) *The terms of positive theology* have a more complicated logic. We learn their meaning through the "method of contrasts." The notion of unity operative in "God is one" is understood by means of the presentation of situations in which various kinds of diversity are experienced. We then attempt to overcome this diver-

---

[12] *Ibid.*, pp. 56–60.
[13] *Ibid.*, p. 60.

sity by relating the "many" out of which these situations are consti-
tuted to higher patterns of unity. Again, we learn the meaning of
"perfect" as it is used in statements like "God is perfect" by the
presentation of situations characterized by varying degrees of im-
perfection; it is hoped that at some point, a disclosure will occur
and one will be led to discern a situation for which words like
ideal and *perfection* are currency.

Positive language does not exhaust the reality of God, of
course, even though it does tell us more than negative language
can. Specifically, positive language makes important linguistic
claims for the word *God*. The idea of unity operative in the assertion "God is one" posits the word *God* as the unifier of all the diverse languages we may use to speak about the world. Again, the
word *perfect* when applied to God indicates that the word *God*
completes the many "language-strands" which are useful in speaking about imperfect empirical reality. *God* is thus a key word that
presides over the whole of language and is suitable for the expression of total commitment.[14]

(3) *Traditional characterizations of God.* Religious language, as
object language, is rooted in the depth-discernment of situations,
and seeks to evoke a specifically *religious* commitment. But this
language needs to be qualified in order to be used for religious
ends. How is this qualification made? Ramsey introduces the notion of a "model," which he defines as a situation with which we are
familiar and which helps us to understand another, and unfamil-
iar, situation.[15] To describe God as the first cause, for example, is
to hold up the model of familiar causal stories as a means of better understanding the placing of the word *God*. But God's causality is not the same as ordinary kinds of causal activity met with in
experience. Thus a *qualifier* (*first*) is introduced which bids the believer to push ordinary causal stories further and further back,
until a sense of the unseen, a sense of mystery, is evoked, which

---

[14] *Ibid.*, pp. 60–69.

[15] *Ibid.*, p. 69. For an elaboration of his model theory, see his *Models and
Mystery* (London: Oxford University Press, 1964), especially pp. 1–21, where
he discusses the uses of models and different kinds of models (hereafter cited as
Ramsey, *Models*).

leads to a discernment of reality that transcends ordinary causal experience. The word *first,* in addition to qualifying the model, thus takes on a second function, since it indicates that the word *God* completes causal stories and is placed "first" over them.[16]

Similar analyses can be given for expressions like *infinitely wise* and *infinitely good.* These terms present models of wisdom and goodness that are drawn from ordinary human experience. The qualifier *infinite* then asks us to take these instances to the lengths at which a characteristically religious discernment takes place: the realization of a wisdom and goodness that is beyond the human and that stands at the limit of all possible wisdom and goodness. The word *infinite* functions, then, by claiming for the word *God* a distinctive logical placing; it presides over and completes all the language of wisdom and goodness that we might use.[17]

Distinguishing the logical behavior of various theological terms and phrases helps avoid difficulties which might otherwise arise. Consider the result, for example, of treating the expressions *God is impassible* and *God is infinitely loving* as identical in function. On the face of it, these statements are simply incompatible, since if God is impassible he is unfeeling, which he cannot be if he is infinitely loving. But upon examination of the logic of each expression, this incompatibility disappears. To claim that God is impassible is to draw attention to the passible features of experience in order to evoke a religious discernment of that which is beyond the passible. It is to posit God outside the language of the passible altogether. But to claim that he is infinitely loving is to present a model and a qualifier. It is to draw attention to accounts of human love in order to evoke the awareness of a love so complete that its better can be neither conceived nor desired. It is to locate the word *God* at the top of all stories of human affection and to suggest that it completes them. Upon analysis, the apparent incompatibility of these two statements thus disappears when it is

---

[16] Ramsey, *Religious Language,* pp. 69 ff.

[17] *Ibid.,* pp. 74–80. See also his treatment of the concepts of "creation" and "eternal purpose", the latter including the problem of evil, pp. 80 ff.

realized that for all their grammatical similarities, their functions are different.[18]

Christ and Christian Religious Language

A parallel line of development, but one which concentrates on the place of Christ in Christian religious discourse rather than on the syntactical characteristics of the sentences composing this discourse, has been proposed by I. M. Crombie.[19] About a religious or theological statement such as "God is love," two sets of problems arise: (1) questions bearing on the *subject* of the sentence, about how we come to know that about which we are speaking; and (2) questions bearing on the *predicate* of the sentence, about why we use it and about what we mean by saying what we say.

(1) One of the sources of religious belief is what Crombie calls "undifferentiated theism." [20] Many men have a sense of contingency, a conviction that obligation is rooted in a transcendent ground, cosmic design in a transcendent designer, and religious experience in a transcendent object. These senses or convictions are not like the conclusions of arguments, but are more like "seeing, as it were, through a gap in the rolling mists of argument. . . ." [21] One is not persuaded, consequently, to believe in one's contingency, but feels instead that it is only by persuasion that one could believe anything else. Such convictions are responses to elements in experience and "provide us with a 'meaning' for the word 'God'," [22] a category of the divine, a direction to which we can refer the terms we use in speaking of God.[23] The conviction of the contrasts between contingency and necessity, obligation and

---

[18] *Ibid.,* pp. 101–102.

[19] In Flew, *New Essays,* pp. 109–130. His position is elaborated in Basil Mitchell, ed., *Faith and Logic* (London: George Allen and Unwin, Ltd., 1957), pp. 31–83.

[20] Flew, *New Essays,* p. 111.

[21] *Ibid.,* p. 113.

[22] *Ibid.,* p. 116.

[23] For discussions of Crombie's position on how we come to know the meaning of the word "God," see Kai Nielsen, "On Fixing the Reference Range of 'God'," *Religious Studies,* II (1966), pp. 13–36; and Dom Illyd Trethowan, "In Defence of Theism—A Reply to Kai Nielsen," *Ibid.,* pp. 37–48.

its transcendent ground, goodness and its transcendent goal, thus gives us a referent for the term *God* by bidding us to refer statements in which that term appears beyond our experience of contingency, of obligation, or of ordinary goodness.

(2) Undifferentiated theism would remain passive, leaving us without active belief in God, were it not for the fact that the believer finds that there are certain events which can be interpreted theophanically. Religious belief thus involves treating certain events as revelatory of God; for Christian religion, the statements made about these events, and about God, are made primarily on the authority of Christ, who is God's Word. In this way we move from the subject of religious statements to their predicate, to what is said about the subject.

On Crombie's interpretation, the words used with reference to God—love, justice, mercy, and the like—are "parables." [24] They are not metaphors. To say that God is just is not like saying that Jones is hot-tempered. For to use the word *hot* in reference to Jones' temper is defensible only because we know both ends of the metaphorical transfer. We know, that is, something about Jones' temper and about various temperatures, and about their effects and manifestations; we can thus find a certain appropriateness in the word *hot* as applied to Jones' temper. But while we know something about justice in its ordinary human manifestations (we know, that is, something about one end of the proposed transfer), God's transcendence over experienced reality precludes us from claiming to know the other end of the transfer. Nor can we do full justice to the meaning of the God-referred predicates by erecting a scale and whittling away one end of it, purifying our terms from all nondivine connotations and, so cleansed, using the term to speak of God. For example, we might set up for the word *activity* a scale in which inanimate matter is at the bottom and human activities (thought, etc.) are at the top. We would then strip away from the idea of human activity whatever it has in common with activities like physical activity which are below it on the scale.

---

[24] Flew, *New Essays,* p. 118.

Having removed from the human residue the negative features like error and incomplete knowledge which are so often associated with human thinking, we would apply the thus-distilled meaning to God and so be able to speak of divine activity. This sort of technique has the advantage of showing what meanings of the term we use do not apply to God. But what is left after all nonapplicable features have been removed is but a "ghostly and evacuated" concept, too tenuous and elusive to convey fully the meanings of the terms we do use in theological discourse.[25]

According to Crombie's parable view, the words said about God are ordinary words, used in ordinary ways. But we do not suppose that they are "strictly true" of God, and in fact, "We do not even know how much of them applies." [26] On what basis, then, do we use them? On the authority of Christ, for they are "authorized parables" which we trust because we trust Christ and have faith in him as God's authentic Word. The believer therefore knows that "God is love" is a right statement, although he cannot claim to know *how* it is right; that is, he does not claim to know what divine love is like. He believes that the word *love,* drawn from human contexts, is proper to use in speaking of God because Christ has sanctioned the use of the term. He realizes, through it all, that the word is not being employed in a literal manner, and when challenged to specify what he means precisely, he will most likely fall back on an incomplete agnosticism—incomplete because while he doesn't know how his words mean, he is confident that they are the right ones to employ.[27]

There is a difficulty to be encountered, however, in that to say that one is loved by a human being is to preclude the possibility of "being let down right and left." [28] But assertions of God's love do

---

[25] *Ibid.,* pp. 120–122.

[26] *Ibid.,* p. 122.

[27] *Ibid.,* pp. 127–128. Willem Zuurdeeg speaks thus of all confessional and theological language as *convictional* language. "Convictional language is characterized by the prominence of a *convictor,* a somebody or something, a god or a cause who overcomes man." So overcome, a man sees his life in a certain way and relates all to his convictor. See Willem Zuurdeeg, "The Nature of Theological Language," *The Journal of Religion,* XL (1960), pp. 1 ff.

[28] Flew, *New Essays,* p. 129.

not guarantee that this won't happen—as, in fact, it does! And in the face of the discrepancy between human love and divine love, it is hard to believe that "God loves us" is a statement about sober fact. This objection, Crombie believes, involves the whole problem of religion. The believer does not run from it or attempt to bluff his way out. But he has his "prepared positions" to which he retreats; and if these are taken, "then he must surrender." His fortresses are these: (1) He looks for the resurrection of the dead when we shall see "all of the picture," and he believes that the parts of the picture which we do not yet see determine the design of the picture as a whole.[29] (2) In Christ he sees the verification and specification of divine love, what sort it is, and what sorts of benefits God gives us. In the New Testament scale of values as taught by Christ, physical death and spiritual mortification ("being let down right and left") are part of the price the believer is asked to pay to preserve his relationship to God.[30] (3) Finally, the believer sees confirmation of divine love in his own life and in the lives of others. This does not mean that he expects to be immune from suffering, but means that

> to the man who begins on the way of Christian life . . . the fight will be hard but not impossible, progress often indiscernible, but real, progress which is towards the paring-away of self-hood, and which is therefore often given through defeat and humiliation, but a defeat and humiliation which are not final, which leave it possible to continue.[31]

Religion and Metaphysical Systems

Regardless of the uses to which they may be put, unless religious statements were truth-functional—unless they referred to

---

[29] Gareth Matthews has argued, similarly, that the Christian does not know what is incompatible with an assertion such as "God loves us," since his understanding of God's love is too limited for him to know what empirical states of affairs are ruled out by it. It tells him nothing about what comes to pass in the empirical world; what it says, then, is that given all the relevant information about God and his plans, every event that occurs in the world would be seen to be consistent with it. See Gareth Matthews, "Theology and Natural Theology," *The Journal of Philosophy,* LXI (1964), pp. 104–106.

[30] Flew, *New Essays,* p. 129.

[31] *Ibid.,* p. 130.

reality, to facts—they would, Frederick Ferré argues,[32] lack their distinctively religious character. But to what sort of facts do they refer? Not to empirical facts certainly, but rather to what Ferré calls "metaphysical facts" of some kind. To explain what these might be, Ferré suggests that facts are never given apart from a receiving and interpreting mind. We accept "ordinary" facts, for example, because they have a coherent place within the conceptual scheme with which modern men relate themselves to the world of common experience. As the conceptual scheme changes or develops, ordinary facts change or develop as well. Today's facts are not the facts of three centuries or three millennia ago, and as we progress both in understanding phenomena and in conceptual refinement, today's facts might gradually give way to the facts of the future. This procedure is true in science as well. Typically, scientific facts are theories that have been overwhelmingly confirmed by conceptually organized experience and by their key position within science's elaborate theoretical schemata. Since such facts depend on compatibility with experience and on the refinement of our theoretical formulation, shortcomings on either side would demand, however infrequently this might occur, that even "the facts" be reconsidered.[33]

It is thus no denigration of "metaphysical facts" to suggest that they are never given apart from creative intellectual activity, but are "supremely dependent" on the conceptual activity of the mind. As a metaphysical system is a conceptual synthesis, "a construct of concepts designed to provide coherence for all 'the facts' on the basis of a theoretical model drawn from among 'the facts,' " a metaphysical fact can therefore be described as "a concept which plays a key role within the system, without which the system would founder." [34]

There are well-known criteria—falsification, for instance—by means of which a scientific system can be judged as adequate or inadequate. Are there, similarly, criteria by means of which dif-

---

[32] Frederick Ferré, *Language, Logic and God* (New York: Harper and Row, 1961) (hereafter cited as Ferré, *Language*).

[33] *Ibid.*, pp. 160–161.

[34] *Ibid.*, p. 161.

ferent metaphysical systems can be judged? To answer this, we must examine the task that such systems are designed to do. Ferré finds that they attempt to unify, and make sense out of, ranges of ideas that would be otherwise unrelated; and that they try to provide explanations within which scientific explanations find a rationally satisfying context together with nonscientific principles of valuation. Both *internal* and *external* criteria can be devised, then, by means of which it can be decided whether metaphysical systems fulfill their functions.[35] *Internally,* a metaphysical system must be *consistent*; inherent self-contradiction excludes it from the rational man's attention. In addition, it must be *coherent*. Since one of the jobs of a metaphysical system is to provide unity in place of conceptual fragmentation, the fundamental principles of the system must be connected with one another. The model must not be fragmented; nor, for that matter, ought it to permit of exceptions. *Externally,* a metaphysical system must be *applicable to experience*. This means that the system must be capable of illuminating, naturally and without distortion, not only *some* experience, but—as distinct from scientific systems—*all* possible experience without oversight, distortion, or "explaining away" on the basis of key concepts.

At least some dimension of theological language—its semantic as opposed to its syntactic aspect—refers to metaphysical facts. Religious discourse "projects a model of immense responsive significance, drawn from 'the facts,' as the key to its conceptual synthesis." [36] For theism in general, this model is composed of the spiritual characteristics of personality: will, purpose, wisdom, and love. For Christians, it is the "creative, self-giving, personal love of Jesus Christ" [37] in whom all Christian concepts are ultimately organized and synthesized.

Theologians consider their statements true. In what sense of the word are they *true?* A theological statement cannot be a literal description, since it is composed of terms drawn from ordinary ex-

---

[35] *Ibid.,* pp. 162–163.
[36] *Ibid.,* p. 164.
[37] *Ibid.*

perience which cannot therefore apply in any literal sense to "ultimate reality." But if the models that we find in human experience illuminate all experience, we may ask why this is so. Then if some model is more adequate than others, we "may begin to suspect that this tells us something . . . about what reality is like. . . ." [38] Theism, be it Christian or not, is founded on the belief that reality is such that the metaphysical models of personal activity will *best* survive any of the tests which may be required of metaphysical systems. However, theistic metaphysics still remains but one conceptual system that provides a possible model for understanding reality. Since all models without exception suffer from weaknesses, man's freedom of choice is left open. But may we not refuse to choose any model? This might be possible for a secluded life apart from the world and the necessity of decision; but the business of living does not allow us to stay aloof. Furthermore, like it or not, a man whose choices exhibit a pattern of some stability has, unconsciously at least, adopted a model which he believes is most faithful to reality, be it "God the Father of Jesus Christ" or "quanta of energy without purpose or intrinsic value." A decision is demanded in any case, a decision "that goes beyond the security of sufficient reason. . . ." [39]

Religious Language and Truth

In his *Twentieth-Century Religious Thought,* John Macquarrie suggests that what gives a "superficial" character to many analytic discussions of religious language is the failure of their proponents to remember that language is a function of human existence.

> All talk is *somebody's* talk, in some situation. This is partly recognized in the new insistence on how language is *used,* but unfortunately many analysts seem to set up words and sentences as quasi-substantial ghostly entities

---

[38] *Ibid.,* p. 165.

[39] *Ibid.* An earlier, and less elaborate, presentation of Ferré's position may be found in his "Is Language About God Fraudulent?" *Scottish Journal of Theology,* XII (1959), pp. 337–360.

> that somehow get along by themselves and can be con-
> sidered in complete abstraction from the people who ex-
> press *themselves* in these words and sentences. No doubt
> some kinds of language are more closely bound up with
> the existence of the speaker than others—and religious
> language would seem to be very closely bound up. This
> means that the analysis of religious language, if it is to
> be carried out with a clear understanding of what it in-
> volves, must be correlated with an analysis of the man
> who expresses *himself* in religious language.[40]

Macquarrie's desire that language analysis be integrated with
existential analysis is, however, largely unrealized. Though individual thinkers may try to bridge the gap between analytic philosophy and existentialism, they are in a minority; the two move-
ments continue to proceed on their own separate ways with little
in-depth enrichment of or rapprochement with one another.

But Macquarrie's point is important. Though there are languages whose use does not necessarily involve the user precisely as
an individual—the language of the positive sciences, for example,
in which the personal concerns of the scientist are formally out of
place—religious language is not one of these. Whatever existential
investigations may reveal of man, and however these investigations might influence and enrich the understanding of religious
language, it is already clear that for the Christian believer it is the
commitment of himself that he makes to God in Christ, his act of
faith, that provides the central motif for his religious discourse.
As Ramsey has shown, such discourse displays varied syntactical
features which, no less than its many functions, need to be distinguished if philosophical and theological confusion is to be
avoided. But like all the language man uses, and reflecting his situation as a being in the world, this language has empirical roots
which are one source of its relevance to human life. However,
Ramsey and Crombie agree that this language has a *plus* that distinguishes it from the other, more ordinary, language-games we

---

[40] John Macquarrie, *Twentieth-Century Religious Thought* (New York:
Harper and Row, 1963), p. 317 (hereafter cited as Macquarrie, *Religious
Thought*).

play. The logical oddities that plague religious statements stem from, and might even be necessitated by, the fact that unlike the sentences of other language-games whose logic may be read in terms of empirical criteria rather than personal concern and commitment, religious sentences find their distinctive character in the believer's trust in one who was authorized to speak of man and God. Evidence that would lead to the rejection of straightforward empirical statements is not sufficient to lead the believer to reject the statements of faith or to destroy his trust in the authority of Christ. Ferré's account, while recognizing the place of Christ as the center of religious belief and language, thus seems more applicable to "natural religion," or to a theism which dispenses with authoritative belief-givers than to Christianity. For the models of Christian religious discourse are not, as is the case with models on which metaphysical systems are built, *drawn* from the facts, but are *imposed* on the facts on the authority of One who claimed to know *all* the facts and who could therefore claim to know the most appropriate models for understanding them. It is not, then, primarily because Christian models best illuminate reality that the believer considers them to be true. He considers them true because he has faith in the Christ who proposed them. The parable of the Stranger and the partisan that Basil Mitchell has told seems to be to the point here.

The commitment that the believer makes of himself to God allows us now to give a tentative account of the word *true* as it applies to some Christian religious assertions. In what follows, our dependence on the work of Ramsey and Crombie will be evident.

What meaning does the word *true* have when applied to religious statements? The syntactic and functional variety in religious discourse makes it highly probable that there is no univocal definition of truth that will accurately reflect what is meant in all cases where the word *true* is used in reference to religious or theological statements. It is far more likely that even within the religious language-game itself the word has many interrelated meanings; thus extensive and detailed explorations would be required before one could justifiably speak of the nature of religious truth in general.

Avoiding, therefore, any attempt to speak of religious truth in a way that would be universally valid, we wish to consider a single statement, "God loves man like a father loves his children," when it is used to *describe* God's relationship to men. Two considerations prompt our choice of this statement. First, much critical fire has been directed on it, and on other sentences very much like it, from members of the analytic movement. Second, statements like this, which draw analogues from the relationships found between men and apply them to the relationship between God and men, are very common in the discourse of believers. It thus provides us with a sample case for much of religious language.

What, then, might the Christian believer mean when, in spite of all objections, he claims that to speak of God as a loving father is not only meaningful, but true? He might mean, we may suggest, that: (1) the statement involves the use of an authorized model; and (2) while some areas of experience are congruent with the model, others, as they are now understood, are not congruent but will be seen to be so when all the facts are known.

(1) *The authorized model.* The believer's situation may be compared to that of a person who lives on one side of a high wall: although he is familiar with the events and relationships that take place and are found there, what goes on on the other side of the wall is unknown to him. But someone who claims familiarity with both sides tells him that certain qualities, relationships, and the like which he finds on his side may be used to provide a "glimmering" of what the other side is like. But he is assured that this glimmering never adds up to exact, literal understanding. He will not be able to specify exactly and in what precise ways the relationships or qualities with which he is familiar are applicable to those others, though he may be able to tell how and in what ways they are *not* applicable.

The believer thus speaks of God and man in terms of the father-son model, not because experience demands or even suggests that he interpret the events of his life and the lives of men in general as adding up to fatherly care, but because Christ sanctioned speaking this way. There are in ordinary father-child relationships features that the believer will claim are not applicable to the

God-man relationship; the best of human relationships are never as perfect as one might wish or imagine. But the believer will point to the tenderness, understanding, care, concern, and love that good fathers give to their offspring, not implying thereby that these are literally true of God's love for men, but implying that these features of the model may be fruitfully used to speak of God's relationship to man, though he does not claim to be able to specify exactly the way they apply to God.

Antony Flew has spoken of the "death by a thousand qualifications" that waits in store for God-statements such as the one we are considering. It is true that if such statements were intended literally (and unfortunately, many believers seem to intend them this way), the qualifications would indeed involve their death. But they do not have to be read literally. They can be understood as statements drawing on models—models that are used because Christ, who was familiar with both God and man, authorized their use. The "thousand qualifications," far from spelling their death, are crucial to their functioning.[41] For by qualification, the believer is reminded that his knowledge of God is never literally true. By qualification too, he is able to exclude from the familiar situation from which the model is drawn (be it father to son, judge to the accused, friend to friend—all the many important human relationships to which revelation points as models whereby we may come to an understanding, however halting and inadequate, of God) those elements which do not apply to God. None of this adds up to literal knowledge, what Aquinas called the knowledge of the essence of God "as He really is in Himself." [42] The God held to by faith is an ineffable God, despite the fact that believers speak of him.

(2) *Experience and the model.* How is the model, which the be-

---

[41] Cf. Ramsey, *Models,* p. 60: ". . . we shall need a never-ending succession of phrases which can combine in pairs to give a never-ending series of metaphorical inroads. In this way theology demands and thrives on a diversity of models; theological discourse must never be uniformly flat. Eccentricity, logical impropriety is its very life blood. The way theological discourse builds up from a subtle selectivity between those various areas of discourse which an endless number of metaphors and models bring with them is no 'death by a thousand qualifications'. Rather is it life by a thousand enrichments."

[42] *Summa Theologiae,* I, 13, 2, ad. 2.

liever accepts on the authority of Christ, related to his ordinary experience? We can sketch one possible answer to this difficult but important question.

There are events in the lives of men to which the believer can point as "fitting" easily with the model of God as father. That individuals receive favorable answers to their prayers, that men are strengthened in situations of moral conflict, that their lives are marked by peace and serenity, that they and their loved ones prosper in their undertakings, that goodness and justice and truth and sensitivity "work" in daily life—all these the believer cites as instances of God's loving care, as what he expects in virtue of God's fatherly care, and as constituting, at least in part, the content of his belief. Does he then believe because of these facts? Do "fitting" observations and experiences lead him to his belief in a loving God? No. For what the believer holds is taken, as we have argued, primarily on the authority of Christ. He does not pick his belief from among the facts, or find his creed suggested as the most reasonable hypothesis by which his experience can be explained; he comes to the facts with belief in hand.

But even though belief finds its ground in faith and is not confirmed or justified by experience in the way that observations may confirm or justify a scientific hypothesis, it seems that there must be some degree of *congruity* between faith and facts. Were human life to become one of unrelieved suffering and misery in which every life was wasted and every prayer unanswered, in which evil, injustice, untruth, and callousness reigned triumphant, there would be few who would continue to speak of God as a loving and compassionate father. That there are lives in which goodness, justice, and mercy stand up to all the evils known to man and overcome them, that there are lives in which the power of self-sacrificing love shows itself as worthy of a life's dedication—these are facts that one would reasonably expect to be found if God were the father of men and that are thus congruent with this belief.

What, then, of those facts that are not congruent with the model that faith provides? These may range all the way from the trivial (minor inconveniences, hurts, disappointments, failures) to the se-

rious (the apparently needless suffering of innocent children, ca-
tastrophes involving enormous desolation and pain). Do they require the abandonment of the model?

It is clear that there are those who, faced with seemingly
needless suffering and senseless evil, especially when they impinge
on their own lives, decide that they can no longer hold to belief in
a God of loving care. For these people, acceptance of the model
depends on a degree of congruity with the facts which is lacking.
But others faced with the same level of evil find in it an invitation
to believe more strongly; for they remember Abraham, who

> when hope was dead within him, went on hoping in
> faith, believing that he would become "the father of
> many nations." He relied on the word of God which de-
> finitely referred to "thy seed." With undaunted faith he
> looked at the facts—his own impotence (he was practi-
> cally a hundred years old at the time) and his wife
> Sarah's apparent barrenness. Yet he refused to allow any
> distrust of a definite pronouncement of God to make him
> waver. He drew strength from his faith, and, while giv-
> ing glory to God, remained absolutely convinced that
> God was able to implement his own promise. This was
> the "faith" which counted unto him for righteousness.[43]

While faith requires congruity with experience, the degree of
such congruence appears to be a matter for the individual's own
discrimination. For some, that this is not the best of all possible
worlds is wholly incongruent with a Creator of total perfection.
For others, evil, no matter its measure, is never sufficient to shake
their faith. For they find their faith vindicated, if not in their own
lives, then in the lives of others living and dead, and preeminently
in the life of Jesus. Evil is no less bitter to them than it is to the
nonbeliever; but they hold that if all the facts were known, if the
sweep of human history were to be seen at once, the Christ-given
model of God as a father of understanding, tenderness, and com-
passion would be vindicated. This is, to use Crombie's term, one

---

[43] Epistle to the Romans, 4:18–22.

of their "prepared positions"; indeed, if the believer's expectations are in vain, he is the unhappiest of men. But he waits in the hope that what he expects will happen and that what he now holds through faith he will one day see face-to-face.

The positivist objection to religious statements because of their alleged compatibility with all states of affairs must therefore be rejected. It is true, of course, that one can tell in advance and with a high degree of specification what states of affairs would and would not be compatible with a scientific statement. This is not possible for religious statements of the kind we are considering. But it does not follow from this that they do not exclude any states of affairs whatever, or that the believer cannot indicate to what he is committing himself by his belief.[44] But such specification is rough rather than specific. It bears on an end result, a future when God shall be all in all, not on what tomorrow shall bring, or how exactly the looked-for goal will actually come to pass. Some may find this insufficient and wish the content of belief to be specifiable in far more definite ways. Were we dealing with an assertion of considerably less complexity than a religious one, this might be possible. But the use of models and the trust in One who asks for faith in things unseen exclude any more significant degree of concretion.

This raises a final problem. Why, someone may ask, is it reasonable to place our trust in Jesus rather than Mohammed, or some other person who claimed to be the authoritative model-giver sent to man from God? How do we know that what is said is worthy of our trust? The framework of this discussion has ex-

---

[44] Cf. Alexander Gibson, "Empirical Evidence and Christian Faith," *The Journal of Religion*, XXXVI (1956), p. 34: ". . . what faith asserts is not that God is compatible with all states of affairs *as they stand* but that God is compatible with all states of affairs *as they are capable of becoming.* There is no state of affairs which is formally excluded from rejoining the divine current, but there are some states of affairs which at given times are not, in fact, carried along with it. . . . The word 'compatible' may be taken statically or dialectically. If it is taken dialectically, the assertion that God is compatible with all states of affairs stands firm. But if it is taken statically, the assertion that God is compatible with all states of affairs is untenable. It presents us with a block universe in which evil is justified, instead of a dramatic progression in which evil is redeemed."

cluded the possibility of judging the model against the reality it represents. Does this not mean, then, that the choice of an authority is a free option, not subject to argument or rational decision?

To answer these questions, even tentatively, is beyond both our competence and the scope of this study. It is clear that no simple answer is possible; many nonphilosophical areas—biblical criticism, history, psychology, apologetics, sociology, comparative literature, to name but a few—would have to be brought into play in order even to clarify the many issues implied by these questions. We might suggest, however, that all men, believers and nonbelievers alike, face an option in this regard which involves a basic decision concerning the way or ways in which their lives may be led. Whatever their choice (for *some* choice is necessary, whether it be Jesus, Mohammed, naturalism, or whatever), it makes sense to look for good reasons, though probably not for compelling ones.[45] If the way a person decides on any matter is not wholly a matter of conscious reflection and ratiocination—for his training, habituation, needs, and cultural milieu all influence and even determine his decision to some degree—it can at least be partially so. A reflective man will be able to give some good reasons for why he thinks as he does, acts as he does, and chooses as he does. Even though the philosopher can help evaluate their worth and cogency, the reasons themselves include considerations that go beyond the limits of his professional competence. Religious statements make sense within their proper framework; whether or not that framework is to be accepted by any given individual is a separate, though perhaps a more important, problem.

Summary

The positivist crisis is past, and philosophers in the analytic tradition are examining religious discourse without, for the most part, the *a priori* biases that vitiated much of the early work in this area. Attention is now being given to the exploration of the variety of religious language—its many functions and its unusual

---

[45] T. R. Miles has outlined what some of these may be. See above, p. 56.

syntactical features. It is now entertained as a serious possibility that statements referring to God can be true in some sense of that word, and attempts are being made to identify that sense. We have suggested that Christian religious discourse finds one of its fundamental bases in the act of faith in God through Christ, and that some descriptive uses of religious statements, which speak of God in the language of human relationships, are said to be true in that they involve the use of authorized models and are congruent to some degree with aspects of experience.

V

Religious Statements:
Analogy, Symbol, and Experience

*"God" is the answer to the question implied in man's finitude; he
is the name for that which concerns man ultimately.*
                    Paul Tillich, *Systematic Theology* I, p. 211.

Introduction

In the previous two chapters we have seen some typical ways in
which the problem of the meaning of religious statements has been
discussed by analysts and analytically minded writers. There are,
of course, a number of other ways in which the problem can be
posed, and as many ways in which, given the overall framework
which provides a context for the issue, possible solutions may be
delineated.

There continues to be a growing awareness on the part of many
analysts of the contributions in this area made by philosophers
and theologians of other persuasions. But while there are varying
degrees of familiarity with, for example, the Thomistic doctrine of
analogy, with the thought of Paul Tillich, and with the position of
those who ground religious discourse in the religious experience of
believers, other lines of interpretation are largely unknown. The
English tradition's earlier hostility to religion and theology, com-
bined with differences in idiom and interest, has contributed to its
members' general unawareness of other schools of thought. But
the beginning of a dialogue has been established. Analytic writers
are, on the whole, attempting to understand other positions in a
more unprejudiced way; insights from nonanalytic writers are
often incorporated into more recent work; and although differences in framework might sometimes present obstacles, serious at-

tempts are made to rephrase those insights so that they may more easily fit analytic thinking. Despite the often heard complaint that analysts are not yet wholly free of antimetaphysical biases, or that they fail to appreciate the nuances of thought and overall significance of the work of many of the persons they read, it can be reasonably hoped that cross-pollination between diverse traditions will lead to mutual enrichment and understanding.

In this chapter we will consider briefly the above-mentioned contributions to this problem made by nonanalysts together with some typical analytic reactions to them.

The Solution Through Analogy

According to Aquinas,[1] religious language has to walk the narrow road between the Scylla of agnosticism and the Charybdis of anthropomorphism. If, on the one hand, the terms used in speaking of God have no connection with ordinary language, we are in effect saying that we know nothing about God. If, on the other hand, the terms used in speaking of God have exactly the same meaning when used in ordinary discourse, God has been thereby reduced to a finite, creaturely level, and his utter transcendence has been compromised. The road between these extremes Aquinas marked out in terms of analogy, a subtle metaphysical and logical tool that could avoid the dilemma by going between its horns.

One of the distinguished representatives of those who use analogy as a means of accounting for the meaning of religious language is Eric L. Mascall, whose presentation of this teaching is widely known among analysts.[2]

---

[1] Texts from Aquinas most frequently cited in discussions of his position include *Summa Theologiae*, I, 13; *Summa Contra Gentiles*, I, 34; and *De Veritate*, II, 11. There is a growing list of works that comment on his teaching. See, for example, James F. Anderson, *The Bond of Being* (St. Louis: Herder Book Co., 1949); Gerald B. Phelan, *St. Thomas and Analogy* (Milwaukee, Wis.: Marquette University Press, 1941); and Ralph McInerny, *The Logic of Analogy* (The Hague: Nijhoff, 1961).

[2] E. L. Mascall, *Existence and Analogy* (London: Longmans, Green and Co., 1949) (hereafter cited as Mascall, *Existence*). Other well-known works on this subject include Austin Farrer, *Finite and Infinite* (Westminster: Dacre Press, 1943) (hereafter cited as Farrer, *Finite*); and D. J. B. Hawkins, *The Essentials of Theism* (New York: Sheed and Ward, 1950) (hereafter cited as Hawkins, *Essentials*).

As relevant to theism, Mascall distinguished two types of analogy: analogy *duorum ad tertium* and analogy *unius ad alterum,* a distinction considered fundamental by St. Thomas in both his *Summae.* Analogy *duorum ad tertium* is "the analogy that holds between two beings in consequence of the relation each of them bears to a third." [3] An example is the use of the word *healthy* as applied to Jones' complexion and to the place where he lives. "Healthy" is applied to neither of these primarily, but rather to Jones himself, the *prime analogate.* This type of analogy can have little or no application in the case where the same predicate is said of both God and creature, for there is "no being antecedent to God to whom the predicate can apply more formally and properly than it applies to him." [4] Hence, the second type of analogy, *unius ad alterum,* must be considered.

This type of analogy is itself divided into two types. The first, known as the analogy of *attribution* or of *proportion,* is analogy *unius ad alterum* in the strict sense. In this case, a predicate belongs formally to one of the analogates (the prime analogate) and relatively and derivatively to the other. Hence, by the analogy of attribution, Jones and his complexion are both described as healthy; but the term is ascribed formally and properly to Jones, and to his complexion because it is a sign of health. This type of analogy, used in a theological way, depends on the relationship of creative causality between God and creature. Hence, the term *good* or *being* has its content derived from creaturely goodness and being, and when applied to God means no more than "God has goodness or being in whatever way is necessary if he is to be able to produce goodness and being in his creatures." [5] This, according to Mascall, does not indicate anything more than that these perfections, found formally in various ways in creatures, exist virtually in God. It "does not seem to necessitate that God possess them formally himself." [6] It is, continues Mascall, "at this point that the second sub-type of analogy comes to the rescue." [7]

---

[3] Mascall, *Existence,* p. 101.
[4] *Ibid.*
[5] *Ibid.,* p. 102. Cf. Hawkins, *Essentials,* p. 94.
[6] Mascall, *Existence,* p. 102.
[7] *Ibid.,* p. 103.

This is the analogy of *proportionality,* or the analogy *plurium ad plura.* In it each analogical term under consideration "is found formally in each of the analogates but in a mode that is determined by the nature of the analogate itself." [8] For example, if the term *life* is considered analogous, it may be asserted that both men and God possess life formally, but that men possess it in the mode proper to man, and God possesses it in that supreme, unimaginable mode proper to himself. So understood, the following quasi-mathematical form is derived:

$$\frac{\text{life of man}}{\text{essence of man}} = \frac{\text{life of God}}{\text{essence of God}}$$

The equal sign must not be interpreted too literally, however. It is not that the life of man is determined by the essence of man in the same way as the life of God is determined by the essence of God, but rather that the way in which human nature determines life is proper to manhood, while the way in which the divine essence determines divine life is proper to divinity.[9] Hence, as D. J. B. Hawkins will write, in a paraphrase of a text from St. Thomas' *De Veritate,*

> while there cannot be a proportion of the finite to the infinite, there can be within both the finite and the infinite proportions which are similar. Thus the divine goodness is to God as human goodness is to man, and the divine wisdom is to God as human wisdom is to man, and, in general, the divine attributes are to God as the analogous finite qualities are to finite things.[10]

Both the analogy of attribution and the analogy of proportionality are therefore involved in accounting for the meaning of terms

---

[8] *Ibid.,* p. 104. Cf. Hawkins, *Essentials,* pp. 94–95, and Farrer, *Finite,* pp. 2, 52–53.

[9] Mascall, *Existence,* pp. 104–105. The example given above is a simplified version of Mascall's.

[10] *De Veritate,* II, 11. Cf. Hawkins, *Essentials,* p. 95.

used in God-statements. The analogy of attribution starts from the perfections found in finite things and, since it is given that God is cause of all that they are and all that they have, argues that these perfections are to be found in God in a virtual manner. But lest it be thought that this allows one to conceive of God in a literal way, the analogy of proportionality serves as a reminder that as the Creator is utterly other than his creatures, the terms predicated of him apply in a way appropriate to his nature, that is, in an "unimaginable" manner. Although the use of analogy thus renders statements about God "thoroughly adequate in so far as they affirm perfections of him," they are still "grossly inadequate in so far as they apply concepts to him. . . ." [11]

Is the doctrine of analogy, on its merits alone, capable of giving a satisfactory account of the meaning of religious statements? The wide consensus among analysts is that it is not so capable, and this for a variety of reasons. It will perhaps be instructive to examine some of the major ones.

It would appear that the analogy of attribution tells us nothing we did not know before. It merely indicates that whatever is capable of producing a certain effect may have applied to it the term that signifies that effect, "thanks solely to the fact that—it is able to produce that effect." [12] This comes down to saying no more than that whatever can produce an effect can produce an effect. But theists then know nothing about God beyond what they accepted beforehand, namely, that he is the cause of all finite things.

Besides being redundant in the sense described above, the analogy of attribution is also excessively permissive. For if to be the cause of something is virtually to be characterizable by the name which refers to that which is caused, then since God is the cause of all things, all conceivable predicates can be said of him. The analogy of attribution admits of no control and allows a whole range of predicates to be said of God, from *good* and *wise* to *sweet tasting* and *finely powdered*! While it may be objected that some predicates are formally appropriate to God's nature while

---

[11] Mascall, *Existence,* p. 120.
[12] Ferré, *Language,* p. 74.

others are not, this would imply that one has a prior understanding of the divine nature, an understanding the analogy of attribution is supposed to supply. "Once again we find ourselves within a circle from which there appears to be no ready exit." [13]

A further difficulty emerges if we consider that according to theologians, God's nature is simple and incomposite, his essence and existence are one. From this it follows that there are no relationships in him, and consequently "the relation of attribution is . . . ruled out." [14] Perhaps, then, this relationship itself is to be viewed analogically. "If so, the theologian is left in the uncomfortable position of attributing unknowable properties to an unknowable being, using an unknowable relation of attribution." [15] The analogy of attribution seems thus to end in the very agnosticism it is employed to avoid. This may be put in another way. If it is claimed that intelligence can be attributed to God only as a finite effect of an infinite cause, and if it is further claimed that such an effect in creatures in some way resembles the divine intelligence "solely according to analogy," this, in the absence of any specific or generic likeness, is "to invoke another analogy to explain the analogy in question, and thus to fall into an infinite regress of analogical predication." [16] As the notion of resemblance here is also an analogical one, and as one analogy is being used to explain another (a process that can go on *ad infinitum*), "the appeal to analogy in the first place loses its point." [17]

The way the analogy of proportionality is understood leads many to suspect that it, too, ends in agnosticism. For in this kind of analogy, there are two unknowns. "The quality x_1 is to man's nature in man in the same respect that this quality x_2 is to God's nature in God." [18] But though we might have a fairly adequate

---

[13] *Ibid.*, pp. 74–75.

[14] William T. Blackstone, *The Problem of Religious Knowledge* (Englewood Cliffs, N.J.: Prentice-Hall, Inc., 1963), p. 67 (hereafter cited as Blackstone, *Religious Knowledge*).

[15] *Ibid.*

[16] Paul Hayner, "Analogical Predication," *The Journal of Philosophy*, LV (1958), p. 857 (hereafter cited as Hayner, "Analogical Predication").

[17] *Ibid.* Cf. Blackstone, *Religious Knowledge*, p. 67.

[18] Ferré, *Language*, p. 72.

knowledge of human nature and of what is literally proportionate
to it, we do not know God's nature and do not know what is literally appropriate to it. This means that instead of the above equa-
tion, one may equally well substitute "x_1 is to man's nature in
much the same way as x_2 is to y." This, it appears, licenses "the
wildest equivocation on the basis of the infinite gap between the
analogates." [19] Otherwise expressed, it has been argued that it is
meaningful to use analogy in order to take an experienced characteristic and postulate it to a higher degree than we experience it.
We can speak, therefore, of man attaining a degree of moral goodness higher than any actually experienced at present. But the case
is different when the characteristic alluded to by the analogical
term differs not in degree but in kind. To say, for example, "God
is infinitely good," is to convey no meaning, for the goodness referred to is "fundamentally different in kind" from ordinary goodness. The only way to avoid the consequence of equivocation that
the analogy of proportionality seems to involve is to discover
some literal truth about the nature of God. But this sort of knowledge is supposedly impossible.[20]

Although these objections, and others like them, have led some
to suggest the wholesale abandonment of analogy, others have proposed that with drastic revisions in its traditional formulation it
can still be used fruitfully for theological purposes. Paul Hayner,
for one, has suggested that any two entities standing in an analogical relationship must have at least one property in common. In
this way the agnosticism inherent in the usual treatment of analogy of attribution is avoided "by the view that what may be truly
asserted about God may also be truly asserted, at least in part,
about things other than God." [21] For example, the term *love* as
applied to God and to the relationship between persons must have
at least one common element. But is this not anthropomorphism,
one of the dangers that the doctrine of analogy is usually used in
order to avoid? Not according to Hayner. For though *love* in

[19] *Ibid.*, p. 73.
[20] Blackstone, *Religious Language*, pp. 66–67.
[21] Hayner, "Analogical Predication," p. 860.

human contexts may have a property in common with *love* when it is used in reference to God, the signification is different because the combination of properties signified by the one is different from the combination signified by the other. So viewed, *love* is not completely equivocal, because in its different uses it has at least one common property. But it is not completely univocal either, because the properties signified by the term in the two contexts differ. In this way God is placed in a class with other things, and this class-membership can provide a starting point for knowledge-claims about him.[22]

Another alternative has been presented by Frederick Ferré, who finds that if one demands that the traditional doctrine of analogy provide information about the real properties of supernatural entities, then little of it can be salvaged. But it is still valuable if employed as one means of providing criteria for the disciplined use of ordinary language in theological contexts. Hence, analogy of attribution allows that a word from a secular context may be used theologically where there is already a ground in the theological universe of discourse for holding that this quality is derived from God's characteristic activity. But this rule also warns that the quality designated by the word is applicable to God not formally, but virtually "as a reminder that within the theological conceptual schema God is taken to be its ultimate source." [23] Similarly, the analogy of proportionality shows that a word may be borrowed from ordinary speech for use in theological discourse only if it is remembered that the word can apply to God in an unimaginable manner.[24]

What, then, is the status of analogy? Do the objections commonly raised against it warrant its abandonment or drastic revision, or does it have a valid function in at least some areas of religious discourse?

---

[22] *Ibid.*, pp. 860–862. On this point, Hayner's account is similar to those of D. M. Baillie, *God was in Christ* (London: Faber and Faber Ltd., 1948), p. 108; and W. R. Inge, *Mysticism in Religion* (London: Hutchinson's University Library n.d.), p. 72. See also Edgar P. Dickie, *God is Light* (London: Hodder and Stoughton, 1953), p. 47.

[23] Ferré, *Language,* p. 77.

[24] *Ibid.*

Analogy, at least when used in helping to explicate the statements of revealed religion, does not pretend to provide literal understanding of God, nor does it operate in the absence of words and statements which are already taken as being meaningful when applied to God, as many of the above criticisms tacitly assume. As we argued in the last chapter, religious assertions of the type we discussed depend on the employment of models; and while ordinary experience provides some understanding of the terms involved in these assertions, this never amounts to literal understanding. Within this framework, we might suggest, the above criticisms can be met, and both the analogy of attribution and of proportionality can be fruitfully used to explicate and to limit that which the believer is claiming to know about God.

When the analogy of attribution is used, it does not propose to tell the believer something he does not already know at least implicitly. The believer already knows that God is the cause of all creaturely perfection, and the analogy of attribution can help make explicit what some of this means by pointing to experienced perfections which "flesh out" what is meant by the divine perfections. No new information is provided; but prior knowledge is explicated, expanded, and better appreciated. This is not, however, "excessively permissive." *Finely-powdered* may be a perfection-indicating term in some uses, but the believer does not use it in reference to God (although he *is* the cause of that perfection) because this is not one of the terms sanctioned for use in religious discourse. Predicating some perfection-terms of God and not others does not then involve the believer in claiming to know what is, or is not, appropriate to the divine nature; it involves him instead in the far more modest (and defensible) claim that he knows what terms are, and are not, authorized for religious use.

That God is simple but that the language used in speaking of him is complex and relational has been noted by theologians. Do we then falsify the divine nature in using relational language, and must the analogy of attribution then be ruled out on those grounds? In replying to a similar question, Aquinas argued [25] that

---
[25] *Summa Theologiae,* I, 13, 12, ad 3.

if we understand God to be complex and composite when he is not, then our knowledge of him would indeed be false. But man understands whatever he understands in a composite and complex manner. Consequently, when he understands a simple thing, he understands it through complex means—by differing viewpoints or by expressing his knowledge in statements that are compounded of subject and predicate—but not in such a way that the thing understood is understood as being complex. The disparity between man's complex mode of understanding and the simple being he understands does not then involve falsity; but it does involve a reminder that the human mind is inadequate to the object it thus knows and can never attain an understanding of God as he is in himself.

We may speak of a "resemblance" between divine and human perfections, such as intelligence. As this resemblance is unlike the resemblance that exists between any two finite things, "resemblance" is an analogical notion. But the analogy upon analogy ends here. For the perfection in question is ascribed to God because its use has been authorized. Although the believer can specify neither the point at which the model holds, nor the exact way in which it resembles what it models, the authoritative source of both the model and the claim that it resembles what it models is the end of analogical regress, since it is the starting point of his knowledge-claim. How the resemblance is a resemblance cannot be exactly described; that it is a resemblance, and a useful one for religious talk, is taken on authority.

Finally, an important function for the analogy of proportionality is to remind the believer that the analogical terms he uses are closer to equivocal than to univocal ones. Between God and creature there is an "infinite gap," so that between man's perfections and God's there is a difference in kind, and not merely in degree. But to use terms designating the one in order to designate the other does not strip them of all meaning; the experiential foundation of the term (which the analogy of attribution traces) gives it an anchor in the universe of ordinary discourse. Nor does it license the "wildest equivocation," since the use of authorized models provides a limit to what can and cannot be said in religious discourse. Analogy, both of attribution and of proportionality, would seem then to have a valid and significant function in explicating the content of religious statements. It adumbrates their meaning in terms of familiar experience, but also reminds the believer that even with revelations he sees only darkly.

Our remarks do not touch on the problem of the justification of analogy in natural theology; that would bring in far-reaching issues of epistemological and metaphysical complexity, whose investigation is far beyond the scope of this study. But if the above difficulties with analogy can be resolved or avoided by the natural theologian, it is still doubtful whether English-speaking philosophers in general, especially those still under positivist influence, will ever overcome their scepticism about its value in providing man with natural knowledge of God. The traditional teaching concerning analogy seems to many to be inseparably bound to a number of metaphysical positions, such as the analogy of being, the nature of causality, and a theory of universals; and these are often found unacceptable for reasons which in many cases do not involve prejudices against metaphysics in general. Hence, John MacIntyre writes:

> Can any of us adopt the Thomistic distinctions between the different varieties of analogy and escape the metaphysical consequences with which in St. Thomas and in all Roman Catholic theology the logical forms are indissolubly associated? What we want is this logic without that metaphysic, and I have the feeling that we may be crying for the moon.[26]

To use analogy in a way that non-Thomistic thinkers would find convincing or even moderately satisfying would involve one in trying to overcome a distrust of it that is very widespread. It would be necessary to justify the Thomistic metaphysical underpinnings that support it, or at least to show that these are not nec-

[26] John MacIntyre, "Analogy," *Scottish Journal of Theology*, XII (1959), p. 20.

essary to its acceptance, and that consequently, one can have "this logic without that metaphysics."

Paul Tillich on Theological Statements

While Thomistic metaphysics may be unacceptable to many analysts, this is not, as we suggested earlier, necessarily symptomatic of a positivist distrust of metaphysics in general. God is, after all, *the* metaphysical being par excellence, and many would argue that a full account of language about God is impossible without *some* metaphysical support.

In the theology of the late Paul Tillich, such support is provided by an existentialist ontology, and the problem of religious language is not considered in isolation from other issues, but is integrated within the broader context of God's self-revelation and its meaning and relevance for human existence.

In the course of his life, a man becomes aware of his own finitude; he "realizes in shock that he is persistently threatened by biological extinction, cognitive scepticism, and moral nihilism." [27] But at the same time, he realizes that he is capable of positive acts of self-affirmation by which he can ward off the threats of nonexistence. This is "the experience of being over against non-being," or "the power of being which resists non-being" and "the power of being in everything that has being." [28] Through ontological analysis, Tillich finds that the experience of finitude thus has a self-transcending quality which points to the unconditioned, the absolute, or being-itself, "the *prius* of everything that is." [29] Being, so understood, is "not the highest abstraction, although it demands the ability of radical abstraction." It is beyond the realist-nomi-

---

[27] David Kelsey, *The Fabric of Paul Tillich's Theology* (New Haven: Yale University Press, 1967), p. 60. Hereafter cited as Kelsey, *Tillich's Theology*.

[28] Paul Tillich, *Systematic Theology*, 3 vols. (Chicago: University of Chicago Press, 1951, 1957, 1963), II, p. 11 (hereafter cited as Tillich, *Systematic Theology*).

[29] Paul Tillich, "The Meaning and Justification of Religious Symbols" (hereafter cited as Tillich, "Symbols"), in Sidney Hook, ed., *Religious Experience and Truth* (New York: New York University Press, 1961), p. 7 (hereafter cited as Hook, *Religious Experience*).

nalist debate, and although "the emptiest of all concepts when taken as an abstraction," it is "the most meaningful of all concepts" when existentially analyzed in ways such as Heidegger and Marcel have done. Being in this sense cannot be suppressed by philosophy, since it "remains the content, the mystery, and the eternal *aporia* of thinking." [30] It is not part of the structure of any finite entity which can be enclosed in a formula, nor is it to be identified with any power inherent in any particular object. Instead, it is being-itself, or the power of being, which is the ultimate ground of all finite things. It follows, of course, that being-itself is not the name of *a* being which, however supreme, however much it may surpass all other beings, is but one object among many. For it transcends all subject-object relationships and is infinitely beyond existent things. Nor can it be described, since as unconditioned, unlimited by any category, it surpasses all conceptualization and all objectivization. For Tillich, being-itself is none other than God.[31]

Given this conception of God as being-itself, how then are the statements of religion or theology, in which God is spoken of as a good shepherd, as creator, as father, and the like, to be interpreted? According to Tillich, most of the statements about God are symbolic. While religious truths may be expressed in a variety of ways—through art, or the language of theology or philosophy—religion's direct self-expression is through "the symbol and the united group of symbols which we call myths." [32] These symbols (true or representative, as opposed to discursive) have, as a class, five characteristics. First, they point beyond themselves—the material of the symbol itself, or "symbolic material," serving as a means whereby what they symbolize may be indirectly grasped. Second, they participate in the reality they represent, radiating "the power of being and meaning" of that for which they stand. Third,

---

[30] Tillich, *Systematic Theology*, II, p. 11.

[31] *Ibid.*, I, p. 238; II, p. 11; Tillich, "Symbols," pp. 6–7, 8, and Paul Tillich, "The Religious Symbol," (hereafter cited as Tillich, "Religious Symbol"), in Hook, *Religious Experience*, pp. 303, 314–315.

[32] Tillich, "Symbols," in Hook, *Religious Experience*, p. 3.

they are not arbitrary in the sense that they can be created or destroyed at will. Although they may spring from human creativity, they need to be accepted by a group or community in order to be able to function effectively. Fourth, a symbol opens a dimension of reality that would otherwise be unknown. Finally, they can have either an integrating or healing power—elevating, quieting, and stabilizing either the individual or a group—or a disintegrating power—causing restlessness or producing anxiety, depression, fanaticism, and the like.[33] There are characteristics over and above these that belong to *religious* representative symbols. They open up to man an "ultimate" dimension of reality—the unconditioned power of being, the holy—and, as bearers of the holy, they produce the experience of holiness, have a healing power, and overcome man's alienation from himself and God.[34]

But although the vast majority of religious statements are symbolic, there is one, and only one, that is not such: that God is being-itself.[35] The word *God* has a dual connotation. It can refer to the unconditioned, the ultimate; and it can refer to God as conceived by religious consciousness. Used in the first way, when God is said to be being-itself, this statement is neither symbolic nor figurative, "but is rather in the strictest sense what it is said to be." [36] Nothing nonsymbolic other than this can be said about God.

> God as being-itself is the ground of the ontological structure of being without being subject to this structure himself. . . . Therefore, if anything beyond this bare assertion is said about God, it no longer is a direct and proper statement. . . . It is indirect, and it points to something beyond itself. In a word, it is symbolic.[37]

When, for instance, God is spoken of as possessing certain qualities, such as wisdom and goodness, and of having engaged in defi-

---

[33] *Ibid.,* pp. 4–6. Cf. Tillich, "Religious Symbol," in Hook, *Religious Experience,* pp. 301–303, 314–319.

[34] Tillich, "Symbols," in Hook, *Religious Experience,* p. 5.

[35] Tillich, "Religious Symbol," in Hook, *Religious Experience,* p. 315; and *Systematic Theology,* I, pp. 238–239.

[36] Tillich, "Religious Symbol," in Hook, *Religious Experience,* p. 315.

[37] Tillich, *Systematic Theology,* I, p. 239.

nite activities, such as creating, exercising providential care, or performing miracles, such assertions are symbolic. For they presuppose that God is an object, which, as the transcendent ground of all objects, he is not. However, these statements contain a negative element, since religious consciousness realizes that they are "figurative" in that they refer to that which is wholly transcendent. In such uses, the word *God*

> has the peculiarity of transcending its own conceptual content. . . . God as an object is a representation of the reality ultimately referred to in the religious act, but in the word "God" this objectivity is negated and at the same time its representative character is asserted.[38]

This does not mean that such statements are lacking in truth. As representative symbols, they open up otherwise unknown levels of reality, and although they provide no objective knowledge (in the sense that they do not add to the store of nonsymbolic understanding of God), they give "true awareness." [39] Special care must be taken with these statements, however, since unless they are both affirmed and denied as their symbolic character requires, they can be wrongly taken as ultimate descriptions. Whatever terms are used to speak of God other than *being-itself,* it must be realized that these are symbols and that what is thereby represented transcends the symbol itself.

How are religious symbols to be judged? The more important of the two criteria Tillich suggests is that a religious symbol is to be judged in terms of the *degree* to which it reaches its referent.[40] This can be determined either negatively or affirmatively. The negative criterion refers to the degree of "transparency" and self-negation the symbol has in relation to its referent. There is, he writes, an almost unavoidable danger in all religious symbols, in that they can bring about a confusion between themselves and that

---

[38] Tillich, "The Religious Symbol," in Hook, *Religious Experience,* p. 315.
[39] *Ibid.,* p. 316.
[40] The other criterion is its *authenticity:* "Nonauthentic are religious symbols which have lost their experiential basis, but which are still used for reasons of tradition or because of their aesthetic value." Tillich, "Symbols," in Hook, *Religious Experience,* p. 10.

to which they point. The religious symbol, that is, has a tendency to elevate itself to an ultimate place of power and meaning, to become an "idol"; and to the degree that it is self-negating, resisting the tendency to be itself considered as an ultimate, to that degree it is true.[41] The affirmative criterion refers to the value of the material the symbol employs. The quest for the ground of all being is man's ultimate concern, and his symbolic material ought to reflect the scope and universality of that concern. If a symbol draws its material from human personalities and groups rather than from inanimate objects, it is of greater worth, since "only in man are all dimensions of the encountered world united." [42]

Tillich's work has been the subject of varied and lively discussion. Theological reaction has centered, expectedly, on the problem of whether his theology as a whole remains faithful to essential elements of New Testament faith.[43] But philosophers, too, have made some contributions, especially to the understanding of the epistemological side of some of his positions. One specific problem that has arisen concerns the determination of the relation between a religious symbol and being-itself to which it points.

Ordinarily, the value of a symbol is judged in terms of its fidelity to that which it symbolizes. But how, by Tillich's accounting, can a religious symbol be judged? As being-itself has no aspects and is not subject to characterization, there is no way of knowing whether a given symbol adequately serves to represent it. The religious symbol is thus autonomous and is not subject to criticism by ordinary standards.[44] A further difficulty is encountered on this topic when one attempts to distinguish, using Tillich's principles,

---

[41] *Ibid.*

[42] *Ibid.,* p. 11.

[43] For discussion of this point from both Protestant and Roman Catholic viewpoints, see, for example, A. J. McKelway, *The Systematic Theology of Paul Tillich* (Richmond, Va.: John Knox Press, 1964); and George Tavard, *Paul Tillich and the Christian Message* (New York: Charles Scribner's Sons, 1961).

[44] William P. Alston, "Tillich's Conception of a Religious Symbol," in Hook, *Religious Experience,* pp. 17–18 (hereafter cited as Alston, "Tillich's Symbol"). See, too, the problems Alston raises with Tillich's conception of "ultimate concern" on pp. 19 ff.

between those objects that are religious symbols and those that are not. For if all things participate in being-itself, how can religious symbols, as opposed to those things that are not such, be characterized as participating in the reality and power of being-itself? [45]

These questions have been generated, in part, by the fact that Tillich developed his theory of symbols over a period of more than thirty years, and difficulties encountered in earlier formulations have, in many cases, been dispelled by later refinements. David Kelsey, in commenting on this subject, has suggested that in clarifying his position, Tillich has changed it on some points. In "an uncertain and faltering kind of way," Kelsey maintains, Tillich has moved from the use of ontology as a means of evaluating religious symbols to the criteria of the functions they serve in religious life.[46] Hence, if a religious symbol is adequate or inadequate to the degree that it represents being-itself or some aspect of it, then Tillich's view is subject to the criticism mentioned above. If, however, his standard of evaluation is the symbol's place in human life, that is, its healing character, its connection with revelatory events, and its function in the community of believers, this problem is thereby avoided.[47]

This later change, or refinement, gives Tillich a way of distinguishing from among all objects those that are religious symbols and those that are not. It is true that "all things . . . have the power of becoming holy in a mediate sense. They can point to

---

[45] *Ibid.*, pp. 18–19.

[46] Tillich's discussion of religious symbols began in 1928 and continued to 1961; his original essay, in English translation, was "The Religious Symbol" cited above; the last was "The Meaning and Justification of Religious Symbols," also cited above. Kelsey, *Tillich's Theology*, pp. 41–42, note 23.

[47] Cf. Kelsey, *Tillich's Theology*, pp. 43, 62, 138: "Tillich does not try to prove the truth of religious symbols independently of revelation by demonstrating the reality of their referent through ontological analysis, nor does he use ontology as the source of precise categories into which vague theological terms can be 'translated.' Ontology guarantees neither the truth nor the meaning of religious symbols. Judgments about whether a putative religious symbol is authentic, expressive, or divine are warranted by analysis of the revelatory events in which the symbols function." Cf. also Tillich, "Religious Symbol," in Hook, *Religious Experience*, p. 316: "The criterion of the truth of a symbol naturally cannot be the comparison of it with the reality to which it refers, just because this reality is absolutely beyond human comprehension."

something beyond themselves." [48] That an object is, in fact, a religious symbol is not because it participates in being-itself while other things do not, but because it has healing power, is connected with an accepted revelatory event, produces the experience of holiness in those who accept it, and is thus expressive of the holy.

Despite this new emphasis, however, there are still difficulties to be encountered in trying to understand some of Tillich's views. For example, one of his more recent discussions of religious symbols and idolatry leaves the reader with the impression that a necessary condition for an object becoming idolatrous is that it must be a religious symbol. Thus,

> it is the danger and an almost unavoidable pitfall of all religious symbols that they bring about a confusion between themselves and that to which they point. In religious language this is called idolatry. [49]

And

> holy objects are not holy in and of themselves. They are holy only by negating themselves in pointing to the divine of which they are the mediums. If they establish themselves as holy, they become demonic. . . . The representations of man's ultimate concern—holy objects— tend to become his ultimate concern. They are transformed into idols. Holiness provokes idolatry. [50]

As we have seen, a religious symbol (holy object) points to being-itself. How can it, then, at one and the same time, point to being-itself and yet "bring about a confusion" between itself and that to which it points? Tillich cannot have it both ways. Either a symbol is religious (holy), and so points to being itself; or it is not religious (holy), is idolatrous, and does not point to being-itself. But it cannot, as a holy object, itself become holy, since its very holiness bars its transformation into an idol. [51]

[48] Tillich, *Systematic Theology*, I, p. 216.
[49] Tillich, "Symbols," in Hook, *Religious Experience*, p. 10.
[50] Tillich, *Systematic Theology*, I, p. 216.
[51] Alston, "Tillich's Symbol," in Hook, *Religious Experience*, pp. 23–24.

What generates considerable confusion here is that Tillich appears to be using the word *holy* in two different senses, as a medium for that which is, or ought to be, man's ultimate concern (God, the divine, being-itself), as well as the object of ultimate concern itself. Hence, when he writes that "holy objects are not holy in and of themselves. They are holy only by negating themselves in pointing to the divine of which they are the mediums," the first sense of *holy* is operative. But then he continues immediately after: "If they establish themselves as holy, they become demonic." This, however, would not be possible if the first sense of *holy* is retained, since the holy object's referential character excludes, by definition, the possibility of its being considered inherently, or nonreferentially, holy. Once it lost its referential character, it could not properly be called *holy* any longer. However, if it is still holy even though it has lost its referential character, this is because *holy* is being used in the second sense of that term.

If Tillich is using *holy* in an ambiguous way, then perhaps his meaning can be construed in the following way. If an object points to being-itself, it can be considered genuinely religious, or divinely holy. But if it loses its "transparency," ceases to point to being-itself and usurps the ultimate character of that to which it originally pointed, then it ceases to be divinely holy and becomes an idol; that is, it becomes holy in an "antidivine" way. In this manner, the (referentially) holy object can itself become holy (nonreferential, itself taken as ultimate), and holiness may indeed provoke idolatry.

However, the fact remains that Tillich's analysis is puzzling and, by the ambiguous use of a key term, engenders confusion concerning the nature and defensibility of his position.

These problems touch on a further issue of great importance. Ontology is woven into the very fabric of Tillich's theology, and its place and functions therein are neither obvious nor as clear as might be desired, even to the astute reader. William Alston has drawn attention to some passages explaining various theological terms.

> If we call God the "living God" . . . [we] assert that
> he is the eternal process in which separation is posited
> and is overcome by reunion.[52]

> will and intellect in their application to God . . . are
> symbols for dynamics in all its ramifications and for
> form as the meaningful structure of being-itself.[53]

> It is more adequate to define divine omnipotence as the
> power of being which resists nonbeing in all its expres-
> sions and which is manifest in the creative process in all
> its forms.[54]

These, and other passages like them, raise two related issues.
First, Tillich seems to be translating symbolic language into non-
symbolic language; or, if he is attempting to explicate one symbol
by means of another, he is not particularly illuminating. This, Alston finds, is symptomatic of Tillich's inability to carry out his
own principles when he is trying to explain particular religious
symbols. Tillich's failure demonstrates the strain involved in
trying to speak of an indescribable symbolizandum.[55] Second, it
provides evidence (as Kelsey admits, though rejecting the interpretation) for the view that ontology is the controlling element in Tillich's work. This would then imply that the "simple believer"
would have to understand Tillich's ontology—used to give precise
meaning to otherwise "vague" theological terms—before he could
claim to have heard the Christian message properly.[56] This is a
consequence that Tillich would, no doubt, find repugnant.

Whatever the role of ontology in Tillich's theology, it is obvious
that in order to master that theology with any degree of competence one must first master the ontology he employs. It is this
which accounts more than anything else for the limited influence
Tillich has had so far on analytic discussions of religious language. The English Channel is not only a barrier to economic co-

---

[52] Tillich, *Systematic Theology,* I, p. 242.

[53] *Ibid.,* p. 247.

[54] *Ibid.,* p. 273.

[55] Alston, "Tillich's Symbol," in Hook, *Religious Experience,* p. 25.

[56] *Ibid.* Cf. Kelsey, *Tillich's Theology,* p. 156 and Kenneth Hamilton, *The System and the Gospel* (New York: The Macmillan Co., 1963), p. 26.

operation between the nations on either side; it has also proved to be a channel of separation between the new world of European metaphysics and the equally new world of English neo-empiricism. Analysts, primarily interested in questions of epistemology and logic, find the newer metaphysical systems to be, to a great extent, *terra incognita.* Many analysts who attempt to read the writings of existentialists and phenomenologists—or to read Tillich—are simply bewildered by what they find.[57]

Such bewilderment is heightened by the ambiguity that is sometimes present in Tillich's use of certain key terms. We have already seen one instance of this—his use of the word *holy.* But there are others as well, some of which have been pointed out by writers who are not unsympathetic to his theology and his aims. John Macquarrie has shown that such important terms as *being-itself, the power of being,* and *the ground of being* lack desirable precision at times; it is not always clear which of the many possible senses of these terms Tillich intends in certain specific passages.[58] As a result, Tillich's ambiguities, especially since they involve words analysts do not themselves use with any degree of professional familiarity, lead analysts to throw up their hands in exasperation and ignore what he has to say.

But Macquarrie has indicated that man's being and his being-as-human need to be considered in giving a full account of religious belief and language—a point to which we alluded earlier. For such belief is intertwined in the very existence of the believer; such language expresses what, for him, are deeply personal and vital concerns. Along these lines, it is possible that in the years

[57] An example of this is William Blackstone's discussion of what Tillich intends by his use of "being-itself." Blackstone's analysis, premised on the assumption that Tillich wishes to use "being" or "is" in some *logical* sense (as analysts are wont to do), rather than as an *ontological* concept, consequently concludes that no such (logical) sense can possibly help Tillich in his enterprise. This would not, of course, come as a surprise to Tillich and his followers. Cf. Blackstone, *Religious Knowledge,* p. 69. A similar misreading of Tillich's ontology as logic can be found in J. M. Hinton, "Review of Tillich's *Theology of Culture,*" *Mind,* LXIX (1960), pp. 424–426.
[58] Macquarrie, *Religious Thought,* p. 367, note 2. But see Kelsey's reply in *Tillich's Theology,* p. 59, note 12.

ahead Tillich's insights, no less than those of existentialism and phenomenology, may come to play a greater part in analytic discussions of religion. How great a part, however, remains to be seen. If the decision to restrict philosophy to problems of language alone without serious consideration of the user of the language continues to be fundamental to analytic thinking, Tillich's work and its European background will probably continue to receive only scant attention. But times have changed and are changing; a reawakened interest in metaphysics among some prominent analysts could well signal a broadening of what they take to be their proper work. The gulf that still separates English philosophers and their continental colleagues may not be quite so insuperable after all. The air of superficiality which Macquarrie detected in early analytic explorations into religion may continue to evaporate as it comes to be understood that man's being and vital interests are dominant, even *the* dominant, factors in his decision to believe and to speak in religious ways.

Verification and Religious Experience

Aquinas tried to show that religious language is rooted in *ordinary* experience; Tillich rooted religion (and its language) in man's experience of the power of being within his life. Still other writers, conversant with positivism, have attempted to show that religious language is indeed rooted in experience; not in ordinary experience, nor even the experience of the power of being as such (which all men have), but in a special kind of experience that some men have had and which all men could conceivably have— *religious* experience. Their position has been variously formulated and has undergone a number of revisions and clarifications. In what follows, we shall present a summary of this school of thought and shall examine some leading analytic criticisms of it.[59]

---

[59] The following account is drawn mainly from the following sources: Frederick Berthold, "Logical Empiricism and Philosophical Theology," *The Journal of Religion*, XXXV (1955), pp. 207–217; John Baillie, *Our Knowledge of God* (New York: Charles Scribner's Sons, 1939); H. H. Farmer, *Revelation and Religion* (London: Nisbet and Co., 1954), and *Towards Belief in God* (New York: The Macmillan Co., 1943); and John Wilson, *Philosophy and*

Although the verification principle required *public* sense experience as a condition for meaningfulness, the principle itself has undergone almost ceaseless revision, and there is now room in the positivist conception of experiential confirmation for *bona fide* religious experience.[60] Philosophers may well suspect that there is something "fishy" about such experience, since it is private and apparently open only to select persons; but it cannot thereby be disregarded. Religious experience is, after all, a special kind of experience and need not have the characteristics of other, more ordinary experience. If religious experience thus is taken as a genuine type of experience, it can then be argued that the believer's knowledge of God is based on the divine self-revelation to individual men. An experience of this kind is so strong, so overpowering, that it cannot be dismissed as unimportant or insignificant for the individual's life. So strong is it, in fact, that the one involved finds that he cannot do other than acknowledge the objective reality of God. Argument and inference are superfluous; such experience is self-verifying and guarantees that that which is experienced truly exists. To speak of it involves imprecision, paradox, and even contradiction,[61] since ordinary language, borrowed for the purpose from other areas of experience, cannot adequately describe the encounter with a being who is *sui generis*. Such linguistic confusion would probably represent a stumbling block for those who require strictly literal use of language, but the imprecision and ambiguity must be seen as the almost inevitable consequence of trying to de-

---

Religion (London: Oxford University Press, 1961) (hereafter cited as Wilson, *Philosophy*).

[60] Some authors speak interchangeably of "religious experience" and "the experience of God." We use the former expression, as the latter might beg the question at the outset, that is, might imply that there is a God who is experienced. Cf. Wilson, *Philosophy,* pp. 70 ff. for further discussion of some of the semantic problems involved here.

[61] Cf. Daya Krishna, "Religious Experience, Language, and Truth," in Hook, *Religious Experience,* pp. 235–236: ". . . it is not that religious people are, or were not, aware of the law of contradiction. Like everyone else, they themselves accept it in many fields of human discourse. It is only with respect to religious experience that all of them feel constrained to question the relevance of the law. It is almost as if beyond a certain range the properties do not hold. . . ."

scribe a unique experience. It can be seen, too, as having the important function of leading us back to the experiential source in which the language itself is rooted. Once this experience is attained, the paradoxes and "viciously muddled confusion of concepts" [62] are forgotten.

An obvious difficulty with this position is that religious experience is far from common. Only rare individuals (like mystics) have reported having it. Like the experience a person might have while under the influence of drugs, and which, no matter how overpowering or convincing to the person involved, is purely subjective and has no objective validity whatever, religious experience would be described by the majority of persons as "wishful thinking" or "purely subjective"; it would not be considered a valid basis for the assertion that God really exists. Some philosophers have put it this way: statements referring to objective existence ("There is a blue object in front of me") cannot be based solely on one's own private experiences ("I am seeing blue"). The latter class is incapable of falsification; no future experience can lead me to deny that I am, or was, seeing blue, since even if there wasn't a blue object in front of me it would still be true that I was seeing blue. Statements that refer to an objective state of affairs are subject to public testing procedures which exclude at least the practical possibility of ascribing real, or objective, existence to that which has only subjective validity. In short, they are falsifiable. But some who affirm the existence of God on the sole basis of a personal encounter with him in religious experience allow no intersubjective testing as appropriate to the case. Neither argument nor inference, we may recall, are germane, since the experience brings with it the undeniable conviction of the reality of God. Philosophical critics have suggested, then, that since the alleged knowledge of objective fact which is based on such subjective experience is not subject to either criticism or control, it cannot properly be called "knowledge" at all. It is not, at least, the kind of

---

[62] This phrase is from Ronald Hepburn, *Christianity and Paradox* (London: Watts, 1958), p. 17.

knowledge that would pass verificationist scrutiny, no matter how broad the notion of experiential confirmation may be.

Two main lines of reaction to the above difficulty have been proposed. First, it has been argued that the relation between those without religious experience and those who have had it is analogous to the relation between a blind man and to one with normal vision when it comes to recognizing the existence of color. Suppose, for example, that a person with normal vision finds himself among a tribe of blind people. The existence of color is undeniable as far as he is concerned, though the members of the tribe might suspect that he is deluded, or that the experience he claims to have is "merely subjective." He finds that the ordinary language of the tribe (lacking color words) is inadequate for describing what he experiences, and the language he is forced to use falls far short of conveying his conviction of the existence of color to the tribesmen. Similarly, the man with religious experience knows God's existence as a datum, and finds that ordinary language is incapable of conveying to others the convictional character of the experience on which his knowledge is based. His knowledge is not merely subjective, nor is he deluded, although from the very nature of the case he is incapable of convincing others of this.

A second approach has been through the suggestion that a testing system for religious experience could be set up by means of which everyone could be trained to have religious experience.[63] This procedure would be roughly analogous to the one whereby persons could be trained to have aesthetic experience and which would allow them both to use and to understand the language of art critics. This program, the details of which are best left to theological experts, might include the freeing of the mind from sense distractions, training in the appreciation of "something general" beneath the particulars met with in the world, and the development of appropriate attitudes as a result of such activities as prayer, worship, and repentance. In this way many people could

---

[63] What follows is from John Wilson, *Philosophy*, pp. 87 ff. A similar technique has been proposed by J. B. Wilson, "Religious Assertions," *The Hibbert Journal*, LVI (1957–1958), pp. 148–160.

have certain experiences—of "love," "grace," "power," and the like —and from these would be able to "construct, recognize, or decide" [64] to acknowledge an entity (God) of and from whom these experiences are. Statements referring to such experiences, such as "God is love," would then be verifiable or falsifiable. This procedure thus has a twofold value: it would give a meaning in terms of experience to the word *God,* and may also "result in agreement about the objective existence of God and other supernatural entities." [65] The difficulties attendant upon the view, which we shall shortly examine, that religious experience is self-verifying are bypassed, since religious experience would no longer be wholly private but would be open to all. An objective procedure for inducing religious experience provides the means whereby such experience would have intersubjective validity.

As some critics construe it, the appeal to religious experience may be stated as follows: I have direct experience, knowledge, or apprehension of God; therefore, I have valid reason to hold that God exists. How is the argument to be construed? The premise is a psychological assertion, since it claims that the person involved has had certain experiences. The connection between it and the conclusion, which refers to an objective state of affairs, must be shown to be warranted. But this cannot be done, since there is neither a deductive nor an inductive relationship between the two.

If two statements are deductively related to one another, one cannot, without self-contradiction, affirm the premise and deny the conclusion. But an existential statement ("There is a blue object in front of me") cannot be deductively related to a psychological one ("I am seeing blue"), since it is always logically possible that future experience, such as the realization that I was hallucinating, or was subject to sense deception, when I saw blue, could cast doubt on the truth of the existential assertion. As "God exists" is an existential statement, then, it cannot be deductively related to the psychological statement "I have religious experience" or "I have experience of God." Nor is the relation between the two state-

---

[64] Wilson, *Philosophy,* p. 92.

[65] *Ibid.,* p. 93.

ments inductive either, since there are no commonly accepted tests which could serve to distinguish genuine religious experience (caused by God and of him) from experience that is nongenuine (subjectively induced states having no objective validity). On the basis of private experience alone, and in the absence of any objective way of distinguishing genuine experience from nongenuine, an inference to an existential claim is not warranted.[66]

But suppose that religious experience is a special kind of knowing which needs no testing of the kind implied by the above criticism? If this is so, certain related difficulties result. First, there is always the danger that even if some religious experiences are genuine, others are not. But how may these be distinguished? How can we decide which religious experiences, and the knowledge-claims based on them, should be accepted, and which should be rejected? Supposedly, the convictional character of the experience itself might be the same in all cases, so this will not do as a criterion of demarcation, no matter how overpowering or personally convincing it might be. Second, without an objective testing procedure, believers would have to give all knowledge-claims based on religious experience the same weight, with the result that one must be prepared to accept the logically untenable position of admitting as objectively true even claims that contradict one another.[67]

The lack of a checking system for religious experience points to a basic flaw in the analogy with sight that has been proposed as a parallel to the question of religious experience. There are many ways of knowing color other than seeing. A blind man may have genuine, though incomplete, knowledge of color through the use of instruments, for example, or he may realize that men with vision have powers of prediction that he lacks. But if religious experience is not subject to objective testing procedures, and if, as so often happens, those claiming to have such experience have no increased predictive capacity that cannot be explained by naturalis-

---

[66] C. B. Martin, "A Religious Way of Knowing," in Flew, *New Essays,* pp. 77–80. Hereafter cited as Martin, "Religious Knowing."

[67] *Ibid.,* p. 83; Blackstone, *Religious Knowledge,* p. 143; and Ferré, *Language,* p. 104.

tic means, then the analogy between the two cases breaks down.

The analogy holds, however, if "knowing color" is equivalent to "having color sensations" and "knowing God" is equivalent to "having religious experiences." But this would now endanger the claim that religious experience is sufficient for knowing that it is objectively true that God exists. For in this interpretation "knowing color" and "knowing God" are equivalent to saying that one is having certain experiences or sensations. Once again the problem of warranting the existential addition "God exists" to the psychological statement comes to the fore. The end result of all this is that the analogy between the awareness of color and religious experience breaks down, since there is the possibility of intersubjective tests, on which rests the claim that color objectively exists, while there are no similar tests which can warrant the assertion that God exists.[68]

Because of these difficulties, the attempt to verify religious statements by appeal to untestable religious experience is far less current today than it once was. However, the version that argues for the establishment of intersubjective testing procedures bypasses many of these, although there are further difficulties which make it less successful than it might be hoped.

Let us suppose that despite the enormous practical difficulties, a program could be established whereby those following it would be guaranteed to have religious experience. Let us suppose, too, that statements referring to this experience could then be made, and that the experience itself is spoken of by reference to an entity (God) who allegedly causes them.

One of the strong features of this position, according to its proponents, is that it makes the rejection of a religious belief or statement a matter of direct falsification. Thus,

> if, whenever the tests yield negative results, we simply tell the subject that he has not tried hard enough, we shall obviously be cheating. . . . We must remember that we are open in principle and in logic to decisive falsification as well as verification, even though evidence

---

[68] Martin, "Religious Knowing," in Flew, *New Essays,* pp. 83 ff.

that is actually decisive may be lacking: otherwise we shall never reach a position in which we can make an informative assertion.[69]

But is rejection of religious belief (loss of faith) that simple a matter? Does the believer deny or suspend judgment on religious tenets because he lacks the verifying experience, or even because the experience he has appears to run counter to it? We do not need to summarize our argument of the previous chapter. It may be sufficient to note that if our analysis has been correct, the interplay between religious belief or statements and experience (whether ordinary or exotic) is highly complex; moving, advancing, and retreating between the poles of trust in one who spoke of God in models and experience which, at different times and in different ways, confirms and/or disconfirms what is held in faith. To reduce this all to a matter of straightforward falsification or verification seems to be a gross oversimplification. Mystics such as St. John of the Cross speak of "the dark night of the soul" in which the experience of God, or religious experience, despite prayer, worship, penitence, and avoidance of sensual involvement, is lacking. By the terms of the above program, the experience of the "dark night" would then decisively falsify the assertion "There is a God" (or "God loves me" or "God is love") or, at least, lead one to suspend judgment concerning its truth-value. Faced with the lack of such experience, however, the mystic does not question his belief in a God of love, but sees it as being tested and increased. What is then suggested as falsifying a religious belief seems, in fact, to be an invitation to grow in belief to those whose claim to have had authentic experience of God is paradigmatic for the religious experience theorists. We might note parenthetically, that for a given individual who goes through the program for religious experience with no result, and who tries and tries again with no success, the statement "God is love" or "There is a God" is decisively falsified—though not for another whose training results in success. Although the program for religious ex-

---

[69] Wilson, *Philosophy*, pp. 91–92.

perience strives to establish the objective status of at least some religious assertions, it does not seem to be able to accomplish this.

There is, however, a more serious defect in this approach. While those involved might be led to "construct, recognize, or decide" to acknowledge a God as cause of this experience, there does not seem to be any necessity that they should do so. It is quite possible that some who have these experiences may "decide" to give a causal explanation of them by reference to factors of a wholly naturalistic kind. They might decide, for example, that the experiences are caused by psychological factors which this program has set in motion. Of course there is no necessity to identify the causal origin of such experience in this way, and some might still wish to speak of them in terms of God. But the point here is that there is no necessity to do so. Much more is required before one can make an unexceptioned case for moving from communal religious experiences to the position that these are caused by God, and not by less extraordinary agencies.

We may put this point in a slightly different way. If there were already criteria by means of which experiences caused by, and of, God could be distinguished from those caused by, and of, other agencies, we would be in a position to determine that a given experience (whether by one individual or by several) was genuinely of God. But we have no such criteria. Indeed, it is difficult to conceive of such criteria being established which would win general acceptance from both believers and nonbelievers. Even if we grant that all or many who follow a given program experience certain results; and that this is sufficient warrant for holding that the experience points beyond itself to an agent that causes it; we still have not made out a successful case for holding that because this is an "experience of . . ." it is an "experience of God"—an experience that would have a number of consequences for the lives of men that the experience of purely natural agents may well not have. There *is* something that many call "religious experience"; but an epistemologically impeccable case has not yet been made for the objective validity of statements about God which some wish to construe from it.

Summary

In this chapter we have considered three approaches to the language of religion which find strong support in nonanalytic circles. For Thomistic philosophy and theology, God may be spoken of through the use of analogy, a sophisticated technique which simultaneously allows such language to be rooted in ordinary experience while still being of some value in speaking of a Being transcending such experience. Paul Tillich points to man's experience of being, as ontologically analyzed, as the ultimate basis of religion and its language. And, for those who see religious language as growing out of a distinctly religious experience, such experience brings to the person having it the conviction that it is "of God," and so provides a foundation for at least some religious statements.

The framework which analysis employs keeps the first two of these above ways from diverting the development of their thinking on religious matters in any major way. The doctrine of analogy appears too closely bound to a generally unacceptable metaphysics, even for many who do not share positivism's allergy to metaphysics in general; while Tillich's position, dominated by existentialist ontology and language, is neither widely understood nor, because of some key linguistic problems, generally appreciated. The program of religious experience, while avoiding any formal commitment to metaphysics, fails to achieve its goal for reasons we have indicated.

But while *frameworks* may cause difficulty, particular *insights* within those frameworks are, or could be, valuable in analytic efforts to illuminate religious language in depth. Analogy, as we have argued, has a useful place in clarifying the language of revealed religion at least, and existentialism's discussions of being and of man's being can provide a deeper and necessary understanding of the ontological condition of those who consider religion a serious possibility for their lives. The program for religious experience may fail to achieve its final goal, but it nonetheless draws attention to the fact that all experience is neither of the same kind nor of the same importance in the lives of men—

positions which, for all its condescension, positivism failed to probe. It also underscores what many mystics and religious persons claim: that because of religious experience the life of a man can be radically changed in ways that lie beyond logic.

VI

The Proofs for the Existence of God

. . . all men agree that He is God whom they esteem above all other things.

St. Augustine, *De doctrina christiana*, I, 7, 7.

Introduction

Unlike some of the questions that analytic philosophers discuss which are of limited interest to those outside that tradition, the problem of whether the existence of God can be rationally shown is of concern to philosophers of many different affiliations as well as to nonphilosophers. The topic has far-reaching ramifications: on the practical level, if it can be shown that there is a God, this will be likely to have important consequences for the life and behavior of individuals; and on the speculative level, it brings into play a number of metaphysical, epistemological, and methodological issues.

What are some of these issues? Recent writers have been concerned with the kind of experience with which a proof for God's existence might best begin, be it the ordinary kind (the existence of change, beauty, and order in the cosmos) or the extraordinary (the experience of God himself which some individuals claim to have had, miraculous events, and psychic phenomena); with whether or not a proof for God's existence is possible and/or desirable; with evaluations of various formulations of classical proofs (whether, for instance, Aquinas' argument from cosmic order is essentially different from the version Hume criticized, or Anselm's formulation of the ontological argument from the Cartesian); with discussions of key words and sentences that occur in some proofs ("necessary existence" and "an infinite regress in

123

caused causes is impossible"); with analyses of the logical model on which one or another argument is based; with criticisms of criticisms (whether Kant was correct in holding that the ontological argument undergirds the teleological and cosmological arguments, for example); and so on. "Can God's existence be proved?" may appear to be a direct and straightforward question, but the philosopher must be prepared to range far afield into areas that may not at first seem involved, in order to justify his answer, whatever it may be.

As important as the above issues are, it will be impossible for us to examine them all, or even to examine any one of them in the detail it might deserve. Consequently, the scope of this chapter will be limited in the following ways.

First, the question of proving God's existence will be discussed as it is handled in the analytic movement, with the work of thinkers of other persuasions considered only insofar as it is, or has been, influential among analysts.

Second, interest will be confined to those three arguments—in Kantian nomenclature, the ontological, cosmological, and physico-theological (or teleological)—which constitute the basis for the majority of analytic explorations. Other suggested proofs, and other versions of the three arguments which are not widely known or widely discussed, will not be considered.

Third, we shall concentrate on a few specific writers whose work has been widely influential and who deal with key issues involved in the arguments.

The Ontological Argument

In the second chapter of his *Proslogion,* Anselm of Canterbury (1033–1109) wrote:

> Therefore, Lord, You who give understanding to faith, grant that I may come to understand . . . that You exist. . . . Now we believe You to be a being than which none greater can be thought. Or is it possible that such a being does not exist, since *the fool has said in his heart: there is no God*? And yet when that very fool

hears what I am saying, namely, a-being-than-which-none-greater-can-be-thought, he understands what he hears, and what he understands is in his understanding —even if he does not understand that such a being exists. . . . But, evidently, that than which a greater cannot be thought cannot be solely in the understanding. For if it is solely in the understanding, it can be thought to be also in reality; and this is greater. If, therefore, that than which a greater cannot be thought is solely in the understanding, then that than which a greater cannot be thought is the very thing than which a greater can be thought. But this is clearly impossible. Therefore, it is indubitably true that something than which a greater cannot be thought exists both in the understanding and in reality.[1]

Of all the attempts to prove God's existence, this is not only among the oldest, but is probably the one to which most critical attention has been directed. It originally appeared in germinal form in the writings of St. Augustine;[2] and after its formulation by Anselm, major thinkers have reviewed it, either to accept it (sometimes with reservations or alterations) or to reject it. In Anselm's day, the monk Gaunilon took objection to the whole project of attempting to establish the real existence of a being—*any* being —merely from our conception of it.[3] Similarly, St. Thomas Aquinas refused to allow as cogent any argument that passed from the ideal, or mental, order to the real order. He suggested as well that the conception of God as the most perfect being conceivable that is the cornerstone of the argument was not universally held as the argument assumes.[4] In the modern period, the argument was taken up by Descartes and met the approval of Spinoza, Leibniz, and Hegel. On the other side of the ledger, Hume dismissed one of its

---

[1] Anselm, *Proslogion* II, in Migne, *Patrologia Latina,* 221 vols. (Paris: Apud Garnier Fratres, 1844–), 158:227–228 (hereafter cited as PL). For translations of the *Proslogion* I have used Anton C. Pegis, ed., *The Wisdom of Catholicism* (New York: Random House, 1949), pp. 208–209.

[2] St. Augustine, *De doctrina christiana,* I, 7, 7 (*PL:* 34, 22); *De mor. Manichaeorum,* II, 11, 24 (*PL:* 32, 1355).

[3] Gaunilon, *Liber pro insipiente* (*PL:* 158, 241–248).

[4] St. Thomas Aquinas, *Summa Theologiae,* I, 2, 1, ad. 2.

variant forms, Kant accused it of being based on the faulty notion that existence is a perfection, and Schopenhauer declared it a "charming joke." [5] In *The Myth of Sisyphus,* Albert Camus declared that he had never seen anyone give his life for the ontological argument.[6] In 1960, however, Professor Norman Malcolm argued that Anselm had actually constructed *two* arguments for God's existence in the *Proslogion,* though he (and subsequent thinkers) had failed to notice this. The first was the one which had been successfully refuted by Kant; the second was another "modal" version which, Malcolm proposed, was untouched by traditional criticisms. The merits of the modal version are still debated today.

There are various ways of stating the ontological argument, and these variants have an important bearing on how one evaluates it. What might stand as a successful criticism of one formulation cannot be assumed to have exactly the same effect on another. Until relatively recently, the majority of analytic writers believed that all versions contained a common element—that existence is to be counted as a perfection—and since this is the point to which Kant objected, his objection refuted the ontological argument, whatever its version. But some have found cause to question that particular view. William Alston, for example, has suggested that Anselm's version, if read correctly, does not depend on the conception of existence as a perfection and so escapes Kant's attack. However, as the Kantian critique is the one with which most contemporary discussions begin, it might be profitable to examine it as well as the Cartesian formulation of the ontological argument to which it is primarily addressed.

It is certain, Descartes wrote, that I have an idea of a supremely perfect being, and that I know clearly and distinctly that

---

[5] Arthur Schopenhauer, *The Fourfold Root of the Principle of Sufficient Reason,* trans. Mme. Karl Hillebrand, rev. ed. (London: George Bell and Sons, 1897), reprinted in Alvin Plantinga, ed., *The Ontological Argument* (New York: Doubleday Anchor Books, 1965), p. 66 (hereafter cited as Plantinga, *Ontological Argument*).

[6] Albert Camus, *The Myth of Sisyphus* (New York: Vintage Books, 1959), p. 3.

eternal existence belongs to the nature of this being. But since, he continued, we usually distinguish between the essence and existence of a thing, is it possible to do the same with the conception of a supremely perfect being, that is, to conceive of God as not actually existing? This is no more possible, Descartes answers, than it is to think of a rectilinear triangle as not having three angles equal to two right angles, or to think of a mountain without a valley. For as God is the supremely perfect being, it is necessary that whenever one should think of him one must attribute to him every conceivable perfection. And since, "having recognized that existence is a perfection," it is necessary that the supremely perfect being must really exist.[7]

Clearly, Descartes is construing existence (or real existence) as a perfection, and since the idea of God is that of a being possessing all perfections, it is impossible for him to be conceived as not existing.

It was here, however, that Kant objected; existence is *not* a perfection or, as he put it, a "real predicate." Whatever predicates we might ascribe to an object, we make no further addition to it if we declare that it exists. Otherwise, "it would not be exactly the same thing that exists, but something more than we had thought in the concept; and we could not, therefore, say that the exact object of my concept exists." [8] To say that a thing exists, or is a being, is not to add something "to the concept of a thing," but is "merely the positing of a thing, or of certain determinations, as existing in themselves." [9] Norman Malcolm illustrates this as follows: If two royal councillors, A and B, drew up a list of the qualities that the most perfect chancellor conceivable would have to possess, and if these lists were identical except that A included real existence on his list, then the same person satisfying A's description would nec-

---

[7] René Descartes, *Meditations on First Philosophy*, V, in *The Philosophical Works of Descartes*, trans. E. S. Haldane and G. R. T. Ross, 2 vols. (New York: Dover Publications, Inc., 1955), I, pp. 180–182.

[8] Immanuel Kant, *Critique of Pure Reason*, trans. N. K. Smith (London: Macmillan and Co. Ltd., 1958), A 600: B 628, p. 505 (hereafter cited as Kant, *Critique*).

[9] *Ibid.*, A 598: B 626, p. 504.

essarily satisfy B's, and *vice versa*. This means that they did not produce different descriptions; A only "made a show of putting down a desirable quality that B had failed to include." [10]

None of this implies that the existence or nonexistence of an object may not be a matter of great importance. To use Kant's famous example, a hundred real thalers make a noticeable difference in a man's financial situation, which a hundred possible thalers could not do. But to say of a concept that it does, or does not, have a real instance is not to ascribe any determination to it, is not to add, or detract, from the intrinsic structure of the concept itself: "A hundred real thalers do not contain the least coin more than a hundred possible thalers." [11] The error in the Cartesian version of the argument is, therefore, that it construes existence as being among the perfections that belong to God.

But what of Anselm's version? Is it to be rejected on the grounds that it, too, makes existence a predicate or a perfection? Close reading of that version, according to William Alston, shows that Anselm does not say that existence is contained in the idea of a perfect being. He speaks instead of a being than which none greater can be thought, which is supposed to have existence *in the understanding,* and then argues that *real* existence must be attributed to it on pain of contradiction. What is operative here, Alston writes, is a conception of "modes of existence," which allows the making of some significant statements of the form "There is one and only one P and it exists" and "There is one and only one P

---

[10] Norman Malcolm, "Anselm's Ontological Argument," (hereafter cited as Malcolm, "Anselm's Argument"), in Plantinga, *Ontological Argument,* pp. 139–140. Malcolm's essay originally appeared in *The Philosophical Review,* LXIX (1960), pp. 41–62. The same point can be put in this way: it is possible to predicate 'p' of being A only if A is thought, or proposed, to exist. Thus, if "exists" is a real predicate, to say "A exists" would be trivial (since the predication is possible only if A allegedly exists), and to say "A does not exist" would be self-defeating (since the predication of nonexistence could be made only if A allegedly did exist). But, as at least some existential statements are neither trivial nor self-defeating, to say of A that it exists is not to predicate a perfection of it. Cf. William Alston, "The Ontological Argument Revisited," (hereafter cited as Alston, "Ontological Argument"), in Plantinga, *Ontological Argument,* pp. 89–90. Alston's essay originally appeared in *The Philosophical Review,* LXIX (1960), pp. 452–474.

[11] Kant, *Critique,* A 599: B 627, p. 505.

and it does not exist"—for example, "In many old legends there is a British King named Arthur who . . . really existed" and "That ghost exists only in your imagination (it does not really exist.)" An object may be said to exist in reality ("The element osmium really exists"), or in fiction ("King Arthur lived in Camelot"), or in the imagination ("You only imagined you saw pink elephants"). Thus the standard argument against treating "exists" as a predicate collapses, since it is possible to set up a subject using one mode of existence ("There is in many old legends a British King named Arthur who fought against the Saxons"), and then, without triviality, predicate another mode of it (". . . and the evidence is that he really existed"). As Anselm's version is thus untouched by the traditional objection (for he sets up the subject, God, in one mode of existence, and then predicates another mode of existence of him), the ontological argument has not, then, been finally destroyed.[12]

But this does not mean that it is acceptable. According to Alston, two features of an existential statement bear noting. First, it functions by setting up a subject for predication. But the mode of existence given to the subject will limit the type of predication that can be made of it. An existential statement is "a license to make certain sorts of subject-predicate statements, and not others." [13] Someone could say, for example, "Ivan Karamazov failed to appreciate his brother Alyosha," but since Ivan has a fictional mode of existence, subject-predicate statements about him, which would be proper to characters who have real existence ("Ivan Karamazov is still alive") are precluded. Second, an existential statement not only permits certain types of subject-predicate statements, but guarantees that there will be true statements of that kind. To say, for example, that there really are sea serpents is to imply that there are some true statements of the form "Sea serpents are . . . ," which will have the logical status of statements about physical objects.

With these two points, the position with which Anselm begins —that God exists in the understanding—can be analyzed. This

---

[12] Alston, "Ontological Argument," pp. 91 ff.
[13] *Ibid.*, p. 101.

statement exhibits logical features common to all statements based on the presupposition of mental existence. These include: (1) that what they say can be conclusively tested by reflection (we need only reflect whether we have an idea of God, and whether it is that of the most perfect being conceivable); and (2) that mental existence has two features. First, for each mental existent, a real existent can be specified. For example, for the fictional existent Ivanhoe, it can be specified that "there are real activities of repeating, hearing, thinking about the legends" [14] with which the character is associated; for an object existing in the understanding "there are real thoughts, ideas, images . . . in my mind which would ordinarily be said to be about this thing. . . ." [15] This is the *real correlate* of the nonreal existent. Second, for a nonreal existent, it is possible to specify something that might really exist which has all its characteristics. This is the nonreal existent's *real archetype*. The real archetype of a dream mountain, for example, would be a real mountain having the same characteristics, and the real archetype of the most perfect being existing in the understanding would be the most perfect being itself.

It is a defining feature of all nonreal modes of existence that a statement about any being so existing has no implications as to real things, except, of course, for its real correlate. Specifically, it will have no implications with respect to the real existence or non-existence of its real archetype. This follows from the very concept of different modes of existence, since if existence in one mode implied existence in another, the distinction between the two modes would collapse. That I dream of mountains with sharp peaks has no geographical importance, and that a statement attaches a predicate to a being in my understanding has no implications for the real world except that I have, or have had, certain thoughts.

Anselm's argument can now be evaluated. If "the being than which nothing greater can be conceived exists in reality" attributes a predicate to a being in the mind, this can have no implications

---

[14] *Ibid.*, p. 103.
[15] *Ibid.*

for reality—*no implications, that is, about the real existence or nonexistence of its real archetype.* However, as ordinarily understood, it has this implication, the purpose of the proof being to show the real existence of God. It would then have to have, in accordance with the second of the features characterizing existential statements, further consequences that bear on the real mode of existence, such as those involving the propriety of worshipping the most perfect being, the causation of the cosmos, and rewards and punishments for action. But it cannot have any of these either (as Anselm wanted it to have). For since the subject is posited in a nonreal mode of existence, this limits the types of predicates that can be attributed to it. Specifically, and because of the distinction between the various modes of existence, it precludes the attribution to it of predicates that involve consequences for real existence.[16]

In sum, merely having the idea of a most perfect being, regardless of what predicates may be attached to it as it exists in the understanding, cannot provide the required grounds for drawing consequences bearing on the real order, whether these be the religious consequences Anselm wished, or the consequence that the most perfect being really exists.[17]

The Modal Version of the Ontological Argument: Norman Malcolm

Although he agrees with the traditional Kantian criticism of the ontological argument, Norman Malcolm has pointed out that in *Proslogion* III Anselm has developed another proof for God's ex-

---

[16] *Ibid.*, pp. 102–105.

[17] Alston rejects the objection that this case is different, that is, that while it is generally true that statements about nonreal existents can have no implications for reality, this rule does not apply in this case which is unique in that the predicate involved is real existence. For the force of Anselm's argument depends on the use of key terms and concepts (like that of predication, existing in reality, existing in the understanding) in their usual senses. Otherwise the argument could "never get off the ground" and would not have the force Anselm wished it to have. But so long as these terms are used in their ordinary senses, it is "impossible that there should be exceptions to the principles" involved, since these depend solely on the elucidation of the ordinary senses of these terms. *Ibid.*, pp. 105–106.

istence which is significantly different from the one he had given in the previous chapter. This is the modal version of the argument, and since it does not involve the claim that existence is a perfection, or a "real predicate," it is untouched by Kant's critique. It runs as follows:

> And this being exists so truly, that it cannot even be thought not to exist. Assuredly, it is possible to think of something that cannot be thought not to be; and this is greater than that which can be thought not to be. Hence the conclusion: if that than which a greater cannot be thought can be thought not to be, then that than which a greater cannot be thought is not that than which a greater cannot be thought: which is impossible. There therefore truly exists a being than which a greater cannot be thought; and this is so true, that it cannot even be thought not to be.[18]

Malcolm's interpretation of this passage includes the following points: [19]

(1) There is at least *a* use of the word *God* in which it means "a being than which a greater cannot be conceived." Anselm has thus proposed a definition for the word *God,* and as such, "God is a being than which a greater cannot be conceived" is a logically necessary truth.

(2) Anselm is claiming that a being whose nonexistence is logically impossible (a *necessary* being) is greater than one whose nonexistence is logically possible (a *contingent* being). This is not to suggest that existence is a perfection, but to hold the more complex view that it is *the logical impossibility of nonexistence* that is a perfection, that is, that *necessary* existence is a perfection.

(3) As the being than which none greater can be conceived, God must be independent of all other things and not limited by them. If he depended on something other than himself in order to come into existence or to continue to exist, or if he were limited in his

---

[18] Anselm, *Proslogion* III (*PL:* 158, 228).
[19] Malcolm, "Anselm's Argument," in Plantinga, *Ontological Argument,* pp. 141 ff.

operation by some other being, he would be dependent on or limited by that other being. A being greater than he could then be easily conceived, namely, one wholly independent of and unlimited by anything else.

(4) If we can conceive of a thing, and it does not exist, then if it were to exist, its nonexistence would be possible. If it were to exist, it would then depend on other things both for coming into and for continuing in existence. It would not then be, either in reality or conception, an unlimited and independent being.

(5) As a result, God's existence is either logically necessary or logically impossible. For when dealing with the existence of any being, there are three alternatives:

(a) that its existence is impossible;
(b) that its existence is contingent;
(c) that its existence is necessary.

The net effect of the above considerations has been that there is no possibility that God is a contingent being. If he were, or even could be such, he would not be the being than which none greater could be thought. Consequently, his existence is either logically impossible or logically necessary. If he exists, he exists necessarily and cannot not exist; and if he does not exist, it is impossible for him ever to exist.

(6) But the only way to show that God's existence is logically impossible is to show that the concept of God as the most perfect being conceivable is either self-contradictory or absurd. However, Malcolm holds that neither of these is the case.

(7) Consequently, God exists and exists necessarily.

Among the critics of Malcolm's defense of the modal version of the argument, Professor Paul Henle has developed three interrelated lines of criticism.[20]

First, a *reductio ad absurdum*.[21] Malcolm, Henle argues, has se-

---

[20] Paul Henle, "Uses of the Ontological Argument," in Plantinga, *Ontological Argument*, pp. 172–180. Henle's essay originally appeared in *The Philosophical Review*, LXX (1961), pp. 102–109.

[21] *Ibid.*, pp. 173–174.

lected as the focus of his argument the conception of a being who is unlimited and independent in the sense that he necessarily exists. Neo-Platonic metaphysics would identify necessary existence with complete perfection (including omniscience and omnipotence), but Malcolm has not argued on a neo-Platonic base, and has not shown the connection between necessary existence and complete perfection.

Let us then suppose, Henle suggests, that there is a being who has necessary existence and whose name is Nec, but who is otherwise undistinguished, that is, he has only a moderate amount of knowledge, power, etc. Obviously, Nec cannot exist contingently since his existence is inconceivable; he cannot therefore merely happen to exist, or be caused to exist, or depend on something else in order to continue to be, or be capable of ceasing to exist. Nec must therefore exist necessarily, or it is impossible that he exist at all. With the seemingly plausible assumption that there is no inherent contradiction in his nature, Nec must exist.

But Nec is a curious being. For if God is omnipotent he can create or destroy Nec. But as a necessary being, Nec can neither be created nor destroyed.[22] Hence, if Nec exists there is no omnipotent deity, and vice versa. But since the proof for Nec's existence is parallel to the proof for an omnipotent God's, "it is a little difficult to know what to think." [23]

The second of Henle's criticisms is an analysis of the notion of necessity.[24] What might the statement "Necessary existence is a property of Nec" mean? The term *necessary* may have two meanings. In the first, it would modify the statement as a whole, which would make it equivalent to "It is necessary that existence is a property of Nec." However this makes existence in its ordinary sense an attribute of Nec, and if this is applied to statements about God (such that "Necessary existence is a property of God's" is equivalent to "It is necessary that existence is a property of

---

[22] But see below, pp. 137–141 for further discussions of the notion of necessary being.

[23] *Ibid.*, p. 173.

[24] *Ibid.*, pp. 174–175.

God's"), it reduces the *Proslogion* III argument to the one in *Proslogion* II, the unacceptability of which Malcolm concedes.

Malcolm must then mean *necessary* in the second sense, the sense in which it qualifies *existence*. But what might this mean? The adjectival use of *necessary* is common—"Tom would be a good scholar if he had the necessary patience," "Death is a necessary evil." But in such uses the word *necessary* does not distinguish between two kinds of patience or evil—the ordinary and the necessary—but is a "relative sort" of necessity. The necessary patience that Tom lacks is simply the patience required to be a scholar, and necessary evil is the evil required for the existence of life, or for the perfection of the cosmos. But Malcolm attributes to God not only necessary existence, but necessary omnipotence and necessary omniscience as well. But for what would such omnipotence be necessary? Not for consistent discourse or for the existence of God, because this would simply be an indirect way of saying that "God is omnipotent" is a necessary statement, an interpretation already rejected. There is left, Henle writes, only the conclusion that necessary omnipotence is a special variety of omnipotence, and one is then compelled to ask how it differs from ordinary omnipotence, and what a being having necessary omnipotence can do that one having only ordinary omnipotence cannot. In the end, Henle confesses to being "completely baffled" by Malcolm's use of the word *necessary*.[25]

Henle's third criticism is an analysis of the use of proper names.[26] As ordinarly used, proper names (Nec, God, John Jones) usually or always presuppose existence. But since in the proof for Nec's existence we cannot prejudge issues by the use of a proper name, Malcolm suggests that in place of *Nec* we substitute the expression, "Whatever necessary beings there are," which leaves open the question of existence. We may then make a series of statements—"Whatever necessary beings there are have necessary existence, cannot begin to exist, etc."—without being tempted to think that Nec or any other necessary being exists, only that they

---

[25] *Ibid.*, p. 176.
[26] *Ibid.*, pp. 176–179.

may exist. The temptation to believe in Nec's existence thus arises, Henle argues, from the use of a proper name, which leads to the belief that what is named exists. But even if the statement "There is at least one necessary being" (whatever "necessary" might mean here) is taken as necessarily true, it does not follow from this that Nec, or any other necessary being one may care to name (God, for example), exists. The apparent plausibility of the modal version of the ontological argument, Henle concludes, stems from the introduction of a proper name, which by itself establishes nothing. Moreover, even if "There is at least one necessary being" is necessarily true, no conclusion to any specific being, be it limited Nec or all-perfect God, could be made.

The Proof for God's Nonexistence

In two of the above three objections, Henle has shown some puzzlement over the meaning of the terms *necessary* and *necessary being*. This is a common situation among analytic philosophers, and it has had some interesting and important consequences. Perhaps the best known of these is the position, put forward by J. N. Findlay, that from an analysis of the notion of necessity a proof for God's *nonexistence* can be formulated.[27]

In order to be the adequate object of the religious worship paid him, God must not only be a being of surpassing greatness, he cannot be limited or dwarfed by mightier superiorities. He must be unsurpassably supreme, towering infinitely over all other objects who owe him all that they are and all that they have. He cannot just happen to exist, nor can all things just happen to depend on him. He *must* exist, and they *must* depend on him. He must be inescapable for both thought and reality: ". . . not only must the existence of *other* things be unthinkable without Him, but His own nonexistence must be wholly unthinkable under any circumstances." [28]

This, so far, follows substantively along the path of the ontological argument. But it was a bad day for Anselm when he hit upon

---

[27] In Flew, *New Essays*, pp. 47–56.
[28] *Ibid.*, p. 52.

his famous proof, Findlay contends. "For on that day he not only laid bare something that is of the essence of an adequate religious object, but also something that entails its necessary non-existence." [29]

The religious person must have a God whose existence is inescapable for both reality and thought. But as for reality, the modern mind feels no axiomatic force in principles which trace contingent things to a necessarily existent source, nor is it particularly difficult to think of qualities underived from a source that possesses them in a supreme way. And as for thought, God's existence would be necessary only if it were impossible to conceive of his nonexistence. For necessity in thought is a property only of those statements which reflect a connection of characteristics or an arbitrary convention, but which, at any rate, do not say anything about reality. Thus, if the statement "God exists" is necessary in that God's existence is inconceivable (and this is the thrust of the ontological argument as well as what is required by an adequate religious object), then the statement has no existential import, cannot be construed as "making a difference," and would be true in all possible circumstances. But if it does have existential import and does make a difference, then it cannot be a necessary truth. The nonexistence of God would then, indeed, be thinkable.

If God's existence is thus not inescapable for either reality or thought, God cannot be the adequate object of religious worship. This forces us to adopt atheism, as the believer cannot have the necessary being he needs.[30]

For many analysts, it is a truism that the word *necessary* is properly used when it describes a statement (a tautology, true by definition), or when it describes the implicative relationship between statements (*q* necessarily follows from the conjunct "if *p*, then *q*; and *p*"). It is improper, or absurd, to use it to describe a being. How, then, is an assertion like "God necessarily exists" or "God is a necessary being" interpreted? Usually, it is taken to mean (as Findlay did) "The proposition 'God exists' is necessary,

---

[29] *Ibid.*, p. 55.
[30] *Ibid.*

or necessarily true." [31] But then the statement is rejected as false or self-contradictory. When, however, it is realized that *necessary* is intended to qualify *existence* and not the statement "God exists" as a whole, the result is bafflement such as Henle exhibited, or the insistence that *necessary* just *cannot* qualify *existence* without the limits of its proper usage being thereby violated.

But can the word *necessary* only be properly used to describe statements?

The *locus classicus* of the term *necessary being* is in the "third way" of St. Thomas Aquinas, in which an attempt is made to prove the existence of a necessary being from a consideration of those beings that come to be and cease to be.[32] There the term *necessary being* seems to refer to a being that can neither be generated nor corrupted. The beings met with in experience— *contingent* beings—are material; they are born, age, and die; they are manufactured from wood, steel, nylon, and paint; they can erode, change, burn, or be disassembled. They are subject to generation and corruption; it is possible for them either to be or not to be. A necessary being is not subject to either generation or corruption since it is not material; but it may be created and, presumably, annihilated, as Aquinas explicitly allows. On this interpretation, God is not the only necessary being. In fact, according to the Aristotelian-Thomistic cosmology, the heavenly bodies and the angels were themselves necessary beings, either because they are composed of a kind of matter not subject to generation and corruption, or because they are "pure forms," or substances wholly independent of matter and materiality for their existence. Even the human soul is a necessary being, since, created as a subsistent substantial form, its existence is not dependent on matter and it is thus incapable of generation and corruption.[33]

---

[31] For example, see *Ibid.,* pp. 52, 54; and J. J. C. Smart, "The Existence of God," in Flew, *New Essays,* pp. 38–39 (hereafter cited as Smart, "Existence").

[32] St. Thomas Aquinas, *Summa Theologiae,* I, 2, 3.

[33] Cf. Joseph Owens, *An Interpretation of Existence* (Milwaukee, Wis.: The Bruce Publishing Company, 1968), pp. 121–122; and James F. Anderson, *Natural Theology* (Milwaukee, Wis.: The Bruce Publishing Company, 1962), p. 36.

For Aquinas, then, and as a consequence of his conception of the structure of material and immaterial beings, "God necessarily exists" or "God is a necessary being" means, in part, "God is incapable of generation and corruption." But it means more than this. For God is not only *a* necessary being, but is *the* necessary being *par excellence,* since "having of [himself his] own necessity, and not receiving it from another," [34] he is the cause of the necessity of all other necessary beings. What this implies Aquinas makes clear. God not only *has* existence, but *is* his own existence, that is, in him, and in him alone, *what* he is (*essentia*) and *that* he is (*esse*) are one and the same.[35] A necessary being other than God can be created or annihilated, since its essence is other than its existence; but creation and annihilation, no less than generation and corruption, are impossible for a being whose essence and existence are identical. God cannot not be.[36]

But have we not now said that the statement "God exists" is necessarily true? "Men exist" may be true or false, since human nature does not have to exist (it is not its own existence). But if God's essence and existence are identical, then "God exists" cannot be false, which is to say that it is necessarily true. This, however, runs into the objection that no existential statement can be necessary, an objection which can be met only by answering that it does in all cases except one, in which essence and existence are the same. But isn't this a barely disguised form of the principle behind the ontological argument, that is, as real existence is of the essence of God, his existence can therefore be deduced from the description of him as the most perfect being?

It seems that Aquinas indeed agrees that the statement "God exists" cannot be false, or is necessarily true. "God exists" is, in

---

[34] St. Thomas Aquinas, *Summa Theologiae,* I, 2, 3, *corpus.*

[35] *Ibid.,* I, 3, 4, *corpus.*

[36] Consequently, and in reference to Henle's first objection against Malcolm (see above, pp. 133–134), Aquinas would have no difficulty in maintaining that Nec is a necessary being (that is, incapable of generation and corruption) but still subject to creation or annihilation by God. Aquinas would, however, hold that it is impossible for Nec, who is not God, to be incapable of creation or annihilation, since this would mean that his essence and existence are one. Of only one being is this possible? Cf. *Ibid.,* I, 11, 3.

Aquinas' terminology, a "self-evident" statement; but with this important qualification: *it is not self-evident to human beings.*

For Aquinas, a statement may be self-evident in a number of ways.[37] Consider, for example, "Given three points on a line, exactly one is between the other two." Within the framework of Euclidian geometry, this statement is necessarily true and is obvious, or self-evident, to all who grasp the meaning of its constituent terms. Aquinas would speak of it as *self-evident in itself* and *self-evident to us.* There are other statements, however, which, while necessarily true, are not known to be such merely by an investigation of their constituent terms, for example, "In general, it is impossible to trisect an angle with compass and straightedge." To realize that this is true, and cannot be false, mathematical training is required. Aquinas would consider the statement *self-evident in itself* and *self-evident,* not to all men, but to those who have studied the subject matter—*to the wise,* as he puts it. Finally, there are those statements which, though they might be necessarily true, are not known to be such by anyone. Let us suppose that Fermat's last theorem ("If n is a number greater than two, there are no whole numbers $a, b, c,$ such that $a^n + b^n = c^n$")[38] is necessarily true, though the discovery (or perhaps rediscovery!) of the proof for it is some years away, or even will never be found. Since at the present time it is not known to be necessarily true, it would then be considered by Aquinas to be *self-evident in itself but not to us.*

On Aquinas' interpretation, "God exists," while self-evident in itself, is not self-evident to any given man. God, whose knowledge of himself is immediate and comprehensive, knows that he cannot not be—knows, that is, that it is impossible for him not to be, and, consequently, that the assertion of his nonexistence is false, and necessarily false.[39] But lacking any such grasp of the divine

---

[37] *Ibid.,* I, 2, 1, *corpus;* see also his parallel remarks in his *Commentary on the Posterior Analytics,* I, Lect. 5, 6–7.

[38] James R. Newman, *The World of Mathematics,* 4 vols. (New York: Simon and Schuster, 1956), IV, pp. 2437–2438.

[39] For Aquinas, there is then one necessarily true existential statement, "God exists." But he would, in spite of this, agree with the view that no exis-

being, the statement "God exists" is, as far as we are concerned, *not* self-evident. It is obviously quite conceivable that God does not exist; as far as we are concerned, the assertion that he exists might well be false. This is why Aquinas believes that it makes sense to seek for proofs for God's existence—a search that would, presumably, make little sense if man's understanding of the divine nature were such that the identity of essence and existence in God could be directly grasped. "God is the necessary being" is thus not a statement whose truth is accepted on internal evidence, which is what Anselm's position ultimately involves. For us men, it is accepted (if at all) as the result of a long and complicated reasoning process which argues that the identity of essence and existence in God is required by the facts and by consistent reasoning.

As A. C. A. Ranier and G. E. Hughes have noted,[40] Findlay's disproof rests on a confusion between a statement that is necessary (Aquinas' "self-evident in itself" would be a rough equivalent) and one whose necessity is seen or known as such, whether to men in general or to some given man. The believer indeed worships a God who is "inescapable," since all that is depends on him for existence and for whatever perfections they possess. He worships a God, moreover, who cannot not exist. But such inescapability is, on the one hand, a dependence that holds whether or not it is self-evident to any given person or can be actually ascertained apart from revelation; and on the other hand, an identity of essence and existence which, if it is affirmed, is affirmed because logic and evidence require it and not because it is manifestly absurd to deny or doubt it. This is, perhaps, part of what Aquinas meant when he wrote that the man who says "God is" does not thereby know what, for God, *to be* is like; he knows only that the statement is true because it is required by the evidence.[41]

---

tential statement is necessarily true, but with the qualification that this is only insofar as we are concerned.

[40] In Flew, *New Essays*, pp. 56–71.

[41] St. Thomas Aquinas, *Summa Theologiae*, I, 3, 4, ad. 2. On this topic, see the excellent study by Anthony Kenny, "God and Necessity" in Bernard Williams and Alan Montefiore, eds., *British Analytic Philosophy* (London: Routledge and Kegan Paul, 1966), pp. 131–151.

In a sense, "God is the necessary being" is not, as Findlay has argued, inescapable for reality or thought. A thinker can study some of the changing, contingent things without being constrained to explain *that* they are, and *what* they are by reference to God's existence. But this does not have to mean, as Findlay concluded, that the necessary being is either self-contradictory or absurd. It may reflect only the less-than-complete vision of the one doing the asserting.

The Teleological Argument

The teleological argument purports to show the existence of a cosmic intelligence, or God, from the existence of order or describable regularities in nature.

Of all the attempted proofs for God's existence, this one has the most popular appeal. There are many persons who find it difficult to accept the world of beauty, means-to-ends adaptations, regularity, and order as things that "just happened" without purpose, planning, or forethought; and who hold, consequently, that the only fully satisfactory explanation of such phenomena is to be found in terms of an intelligence who designed and planned the cosmos. So powerful is this argument, in fact, that even some of its critics acknowledge its appeal. Kant found it philosophically inconclusive, but paid tribute to its ability to lead man to admire the greatness, wisdom, and power of the author of nature,[42] and Hume allowed that there was at least a weak probability that a cosmic designer might be responsible for order and beauty in nature.[43]

Although often spoken of as "the argument from design," it is perhaps more exact to speak of it as "the argument from order." The difference in nomenclature is important. The nerve of the argument is whether observed order provides sufficient evidence whereby one may conclude that intelligence is behind this order.

---

[42] Kant, *Critique,* A 629: B 657, p. 523.

[43] David Hume, *Dialogues Concerning Natural Religion,* V, in *The English Philosophers from Bacon to Mill,* ed. E. A. Burtt (New York: The Modern Library, 1939), p. 720 (hereafter cited as Hume, *Dialogues*).

All might agree without much trouble that there is order in the cosmos, and the question then becomes whether this order is a result of planning and forethought. If it is, and if this point can be established, then and only then can we speak of the order as design. If it cannot be established, then the word *design* (which implies, in the majority of its uses, the work of intelligence) would be inappropriate.

The teleological argument may be put in a simple deductive form as follows:

> There is cosmic order.
> All order results from intelligent planning.
> Therefore, cosmic order results from intelligent planning.

While the existence of cosmic order may be granted without much difficulty, the key premise which needs to be established is the second, the major, one. How can this be done? One attempt to do it was made by St. Thomas Aquinas in his "fifth way," which argues:

> We see that things which lack knowledge, such as natural bodies, act for an end, and this is evident from their acting always, or nearly always, in the same way, so as to obtain the best result. Hence it is plain that they achieve their end, not fortuitously, but designedly. Now whatever lacks knowledge cannot move towards an end, unless it be directed by some being endowed with knowledge and intelligence; as the arrow is directed by the archer. Therefore some intelligent being exists by whom all natural things are directed to their end; and this being we call God.[44]

The argument appears to involve the following points:

(1) It begins with, and it is clearly restricted in its datum to, "things which lack knowledge." Aquinas is not asserting that these things *always* operate in an orderly fashion, or even that they *all*

---

[44] St. Thomas Aquinas, *Summa Theologiae,* I, 2, 3, *corpus.*

operate *some* of the time in an orderly fashion. The proof does not demand perfect, invariable regularity. All it demands is that *some* things operate orderly *some* of the time, that is, that they behave in ways that can be predicted or anticipated.

(2) While the argument states that "things without knowledge" operate "for an end" this does not beg the question, as might first appear. It is true that since nonknowing entities cannot, by definition, fix or select their ends or purposes for themselves, then if they do act "for an end" it would follow that there is some agent that fixes their ends for them. Since the notion of "end" or "purpose" usually connotes intelligence, it would seem that Aquinas has smuggled his conclusion into his premise. However, within the framework of the proof "for an end" seems equivalent to "in a predictable manner" or "in a way that an anticipated result always, or nearly always, occurs." This does not prejudge the issue.

(3) The heart of the argument lies in the following: ". . . they achieve their end, not fortuitously, but designedly. Now whatever lacks knowledge cannot move toward an end, unless it be directed by some being endowed with knowledge and intelligence. . . ." If it can be shown that this order could come about only by design, and not fortuitously, the proof stands. How is it shown? In the above argument we have a suggestion: ". . . as the arrow is directed by the archer"; in the *Summa Contra Gentiles,* the argument is more clearly expressed.

> Among all the things that are ordered to one another . . . their order to one another is for the sake of their order to something one; just as the order of the parts of an army among themselves is for the sake of the order of the whole army to its general. For that some diverse things should be united by some relationship cannot come about from their own natures as diverse things, since on this basis they would rather be distinguished from one another. Nor can this unity come from diverse ordering causes because they could not possibly intend one order in so far as among themselves they are diverse. Thus, either the order of many to one is accidental, or we must reduce it to some one first ordering

> cause that orders all other things to the end it intends.
> Now, we find that all the parts of the world are ordered
> to one another according as some things help some
> other things. . . . Nor is this something accidental,
> since it takes place always or for the most part.[45]

Suppose an army went into battle and decisively routed its enemy. It would be reasonable to suppose that this resulted from careful planning on the part of a commanding officer. But it would still be possible, and reasonable, to claim that there was no preplanning, but that the victory was the result of a series of fortunate accidents. But suppose the same army, against enemy after enemy, wins victory after victory. It would then be unreasonable, though not self-contradictory, to claim that this was purely the result of fortunate circumstances. One, or even a few, victories might be reasonably explained in this way. A series of victories would require the planning of a commanding officer.

Along this line Aquinas constructs his analogy. The various nonknowing entities in the universe exhibit a regular tendency to cooperate with one another in the achievement of some predictable result. They could not on their own do this, since being themselves diverse, they would not act in a unified manner. There must, consequently, be an Orderer who directs their cooperation.

How strong is the analogy? Antony Flew has suggested that the only way in which Aquinas could know that, left to themselves, nonconscious entities would not be united in a relationship to one another would be if he could know what, apart from the orderer's direction, they would do. If some things could be removed from the orderer's direction, it would be possible to learn what they could and could not do when left to themselves. But since, according to Aquinas, the all-pervasiveness of divine providence makes such examination impossible, it is not possible to decide whether the interrelationship among nonconscious beings springs "from their own natures" or requires an orderer external to them. Aqui-

---

[45] St. Thomas Aquinas, *Summa Contra Gentiles*, I, 42, 7. This is the translation by Anton Pegis, *On the Truth of the Catholic Faith*, 5 vols. (Garden City, N.Y.: Image Books, 1955), I, pp. 159–160.

nas is thus finally involved in claiming to know something he cannot possibly know.[46]

There is another way of looking at the argument that may, however, prove more successful. Aquinas has offered a disjunction; the behavior of nonknowing entities is to be explained either by chance or by design, the latter implying intelligence. If a being acts erratically, in a way that cannot be subsumed under some general or quasi-general formula that allows it to be predicted, we usually refer to this activity in terms of chance. But if the behavior can be predicted and explained, it cannot be explained except by reference to the operations of intelligence.

It is here that the lines between those who support the argument and those who find it objectionable are most clearly drawn. All might agree that we can have explanations of the behavior of nonconscious beings, either in themselves or in relation to one another, which do not involve, at early levels, reference to intelligent planning. One may, for example, find a satisfactory explanation of the eye's seeing without calling into play an ultimate designer of rods and cones. But the argument's supporters would want to urge that this explanation, though adequate as far as it goes, does not go far enough. For can we rest content with explanations of order, regularity, etc. that stop short of an "ultimate why" of them? A given bit of ordered behavior might be intelligible within a general framework of explanation, but unless there is an ultimate explanation for all such piecemeal explanations, an ultimate explanation for the very *framework of explanation itself,* we are holding, in the end, that the cosmos is radically unintelligible.

Responses to this line of argument come from different quarters. First, *from the nature of explanations.* The argument's supporters refuse to be content with explanations that leave off, or are not ultimate. This is understandable. No one can be fully satisfied with an explanation that raises further questions for which no answers are yet found. But is reference to a cosmic orderer, as such, a satisfying way of ending explanations? Surely there are

---

[46] Antony Flew, *God and Philosophy* (New York: Harcourt, Brace and World, Inc., 1966), pp. 70–72 (hereafter cited as Flew, *God*).

questions that may still be asked—why the orderer chose this design rather than another, why he has not included more order than he actually has—which are unanswered by even this "ultimate" explanation.[47]

Second, *from the supposed unintelligibility of the cosmos.*[48] It is urged that without an ultimate explanation the cosmos would be unintelligible. Put in another way, it can be urged that the regularities in the cosmos cannot be the result of chance. There are two related replies to this. First, to say the cosmos is intelligible as a whole is another way of saying that it is the result of intelligent planning, that is, that it has an Orderer. Conversely, to deny that the cosmos is intelligible as a whole is part of the denial that it has an Orderer. It would then be begging the question to say that since the cosmos is intelligible, it therefore has an Orderer. It *may* be intelligible as a whole, or it *may* have an Orderer; but no one of these assertions can be used as a premise by means of which the other is concluded. Second, and in the words of C. S. Peirce, "Universes are not as plentiful as blackberries." [49] The very uniqueness of the cosmos destroys the basis for the usual contrast between chance and design. While it may be licit to speak, within the framework of experience, of this contrast, when the entire framework is in question—a framework that we have never experienced as a whole—whether the contrast still holds is, at best, debatable, and at worst, it breaks down altogether. As Flew writes, "It is, therefore, not a matter here of having to choose between the prongs of either fork. Instead the difficulty is to appreciate that and why neither choice can arise." [50]

---

[47] *Ibid.*, p. 83. Some writers hold that to explain events in terms of a supernatural agency tends to stifle further enquiry, since it implies that any other way of explanation that may be tried is unpromising: "In the interests of knowledge we have a duty never to stipulate this way." T. R. Miles, "On Excluding the Supernatural," *Religious Studies,* I (1965), p. 147 (hereafter cited as Miles, "Excluding"). Note also p. 150, in which Miles seems to have modified his stand on the meaning of religious statements (cf. above, chap. III, p. 4) in the direction of Ramsey's view.

[48] Flew, *God,* pp. 69–70, 74.

[49] Quoted in *Ibid.*, p. 74. I have been unable to find the source in Peirce.

[50] *Ibid.*, p. 74.

Third, *from the analogy underlying the argument.* Defenders of the teleological argument require an ultimate explanation of all explanations of cosmic order. But must there be such an explanation? What is behind the requirement, the argument's critics believe, is an analogy between cosmic order and works and activities springing from human intelligence (thus the analogy of the arrow and its target, the army's victories and its commander). But how strong is this analogy? Critics fall back on Hume's *Dialogues Concerning Natural Religion,* in which one version of the argument is subjected to detailed criticism.[51] Hume argued that while we can infer that a half-built house has an architect because we have had direct experience of the origins of other, and similar, buildings, we have no direct experience of the origin of the universe, and so lack the required basis for claiming that *this* universe arose from the operations of intelligence. However, if it is suggested that the parts of the universe which we directly experience are sufficiently like works of human making (machines, for example) to allow us to infer that the cosmos as a whole has an intelligent designer analogous to the human designer of a machine, Hume counters that this type of reasoning goes from part to whole. As we do not allow such reasoning in other matters (we cannot, for instance, draw a conclusion about human generation from watching the growth of a hair), we cannot therefore use it here. Furthermore, Hume maintains, while it might be allowed that our experience of machines and other like works provides a model which has value in understanding the universe, there are other objects in experience (animals, vegetables) that can also provide a model for a similar understanding of the universe as a whole. But this leads to ridiculous results. For example, we could then argue that as animals and vegetables arise by generation and vegetation, so the universe arose in a similar way. The universe of order and harmony may be the result of intelligent planning; it may have arisen because its material elements just happened to fall into a particular pattern. But as we have not witnessed the origins, development, and destruction of universes, any of these suppositions which are drawn

---

[51] For the Humean criticism, see Hume, *Dialogues,* II, V, VII, XI.

from our limited experience is equally possible. The analogue with works and activities of human intelligence which underlies the argument from order is thus not strong enough to support with any significant degree of probability the statement that a cosmic intelligence exists.

The Cosmological Argument

The "cosmological argument" is the name that ambiguously designates a group of arguments for God's existence which take as their starting point the existence of contingent beings (or changing beings, or conditioned beings, or beings who are efficient causes), and attempt to prove thereby the existence of a necessary being (or an unchanging being, an unconditioned being, a first efficient cause). In the form in which it was criticized by Kant, it may be found in "Principles of Nature and Grace . . . ," an essay in which Leibniz, invoking what he called the "great principle" that *nothing takes place without sufficient reason,* felt entitled to ask, "Why is there something rather than nothing?" To suppose, further, that things must exist, it must be possible to give a reason why they exist just as they do and not in some other manner. But this sufficient reason cannot be found in the series of contingent things.

> For since matter is in itself indifferent to motion or to rest, and to one motion rather than another, it cannot itself contain the reason of motion, still less of a particular motion. And although the present motion which is in matter arises from the one before it, and this in its turn from the one before that, we are no further on however far we go; for the same question always remains. Thus the sufficient reason, which needs no further reason, must be outside this series of contingent things, and must lie in a substance which is the cause of this series, or which is a being that bears the reason of its existence within itself; otherwise we should still not have a sufficient reason, with which we could stop. And this final reason of things is called *God.*[52]

---

[52] G. W. Leibniz, "Principles of Nature and Grace . . . ," section 8, in *Leibniz: Philosophical Writings,* trans. Mary Morris (London: J. M. Dent and Sons Ltd., 1934), p. 26.

Another argument, also called the cosmological argument, is the "third way" of St. Thomas Aquinas—the argument from possibility and necessity, as he called it. Further, it is widely held by analytic writers that the first two ways that Aquinas gives—the arguments from motion and from efficient causation—are essentially the same as the third, although they start from a different aspect of things.

Granted the importance of the argument, whatever its version in different philosophical traditions, it has only recently begun to be widely discussed by analytic writers. The reasons for this are not hard to find. The positivist climate led many to ignore it, since it was a piece of metaphysics and so meaningless. But whenever the subject may have been discussed, most thinkers fell back on Kant, who had held that the cosmological argument needed to be completed by the ontological argument. But since this latter was invalid, the former was thereby disposed of. The positivist attitude has given way to greater receptivity to metaphysics, however, and Kant's criticism has itself been subject to criticisms which, subsequently, also came under fire. There is interest, too, in the scrutinization of the argument in versions other than the Leibnizian, the one with which Kant was familiar. In his recent *God and Other Minds,* Alvin Plantinga selects Aquinas' third way for serious, detailed analysis, concluding on grounds far too elaborate to be presented here, that it is "ineffective." [53] Antony Flew, in his *God and Philosophy,* gives separate consideration to the argument from efficient causation as the Thomistic version of the cosmological argument "most immediately intelligible and forceful to the modern student. . . ." [54] No doubt the realization that the death of the Cartesian ontological argument did not invalidate all forms of the ontological argument has led, in this case as well, to greater caution about making general critiques.

In his criticism of the cosmological argument, J. J. C. Smart has suggested that Kant had made a "very simple mistake" [55] in ele-

---

[53] Alvin Plantinga, *God and Other Minds* (New York: Cornell University Press, 1967), p. 25. For his complete discussion of the proof, see pp. 3–25.

[54] Flew, *God,* p. 87.

[55] Smart, "Existence," in Flew, *New Essays,* p. 37.

mentary logic and had, besides, mislocated the focus of the trouble besetting the argument.

As Kant read the argument, it has two parts. The first, in summary, would go:

> If anything exists, an absolutely necessary being must also exist.
> Now I, at least, exist.
> Therefore, an absolutely necessary being exists.

The argument then proceeds to show that the absolutely necessary being must be an infinitely perfect being; and *this,* Kant claimed, was merely the ontological argument all over again. For the statement "All necessary beings are infinitely perfect beings" implies that "Some infinitely perfect beings are necessarily existent beings." But as there can be only one such being, we may replace the latter statement with "All infinitely perfect beings are necessarily existent beings." This last will be recognized as the principle of the ontological argument.[56]

Where was Kant's mistake? He had forgotten, Smart suggests, that the existence of a necessary being had already been allegedly proved in the first part of the argument. His changing of "All necessary beings are infinitely perfect beings" to "Some infinitely perfect beings are necessarily existent beings" is valid only if the existence of a necessary being is presupposed. But Kant was misled in an ambiguity in the word "all" which may take for granted the existence of the subject so quantified ("All who are reading these lines have nothing better to do"), but which may not ("All trespassers will be prosecuted," which means only "If there are any trespassers, they will be prosecuted"). In his criticism, Kant uses the word "all" sometimes in one sense and sometimes in the other. "So," Smart concludes, "Kant's criticism won't do."[57]

What, then, is wrong with the argument? The problem, for Smart, is located in the *first* part, which concludes with the existence of a necessary being. "And by 'a necessary being' the cos-

---

[56] For Kant's criticism, cf. *Critique,* A 603: B 631 ff., pp. 507 ff.
[57] Smart, "Existence," in Flew, *New Essays,* p. 37.

mological argument means 'a *logically* necessary being,' i.e., 'a being whose nonexistence is inconceivable in the sort of way that a triangle's having four sides is inconceivable'." [58] However, he continues (in lines now quite familiar), necessity is a property of propositions, not of beings. Hence "God is a necessary being" must be equivalent to "The proposition 'God exists' is necessary." But, of course, no existential proposition can be necessary. It is thus impossible to have a logically necessary being. "We reject the cosmological argument, then, because it rests on a thorough absurdity." [59]

But does it? It is simply false to assert that "by 'a necessary being' the cosmological argument means . . . 'a being whose nonexistence is inconceivable *in the sort of way that a triangle's having four sides is inconceivable'."* At least, and as we have seen earlier in this chapter, it is not what Aquinas means when he holds that God is *the* necessary being *par excellence,* or that the statement "God exists" is necessarily true. As necessarily true in itself, but not to us, he did not hold that God's nonexistence is inconceivable at all. As Henry Veatch puts it, in a somewhat rough manner, "the statement 'God exists' or 'A necessary being exists,' taken as the conclusion of a cosmological type argument, is a contingent truth; it is not a logically necessary one." [60] Whether or not the cosmological argument, at least in the "third way" version of Aquinas, establishes the existence of a necessary being, it does not seem justified to reject it on the grounds marked out by Smart.

Another point of interest in the argument is the statement that in tracing the ordered series of contingent beings (moving beings, caused causes, or whatever), "it is impossible to go on to infinity." This sentence, or one very similar to it, occurs in the first three of Aquinas' five ways. How is it to be understood? And can it lead to the conclusion that Aquinas wishes, that is, that a necessary being exists? Widely different evaluations are current. On one end

---

[58] *Ibid.,* p. 38.

[59] *Ibid.,* p. 39.

[60] Henry B. Veatch, "A Case for Transempirical and Supernaturalistic Knowledge-Claims," in Feyerabend and Maxwell, *Mind,* p. 395 (hereafter cited as Veatch, "Knowledge-Claims").

of the spectrum, Peter Geatch and G. E. M. Anscombe suggest that Aquinas does not mean that God can be reached by following a causal chain starting from any random object, and that the impossibility means that the existence of a necessary being can be concluded; while at the other end, Antony Flew has argued that whichever of the two different interpretations may be placed upon this sentence, it does not lead to the conclusion Aquinas draws.

On the Geatch-Anscombe reading, Aquinas is not holding that the backward series of ordered contingent beings logically has to be finite and terminate in God. Rather, he believes that the entire series of contingent beings A, B, C, D, . . . etc. can be taken together *as a whole,* and it is thus legitimate to ask about this whole the sorts of questions one would ask about its parts. So, "If it began to exist, what brought it into existence? In any case, what keeps it from perishing, as some of its parts perish? And what keeps its processes going? And to what end?" [61] In thus tracing the causes of a being A, not only may B, C, D, . . . etc. be said to cause it, but, taking B, C, D, . . . etc. as a unity which we may call X, we may then say that not only does B, C, D, . . . etc. cause A, but X as a whole did, in virtue of being itself in process of change.

> But what is it that maintains this process of change in X? Something that cannot itself be in process of change: for if it were, it would just be one of the things in process of change that causes the process in A (or the coming-to-be of A); i.e., it would after all be just part of the changeable system of causes we call X, and not the cause of the process in X. Thus we are led to a changeless cause of the change and coming to be in the world. . . .[62]

The number of terms in X is, of course, irrelevant, and the changeless cause, introduced as the cause of the change in the

[61] G. E. M. Anscombe and P. T. Geatch, *Three Philosophers: Aristotle, Aquinas, and Frege* (Oxford: Basil Blackwell, 1963), p. 112.
[62] *Ibid.,* pp. 113–114.

whole system X, is not the last link in the chain but is other than the system whose processes it causes.

"It is impossible to go on to infinity" is subject to two interpretations, according to Antony Flew. If it means that God is the first in a series of ordered beings, and if that series is eternal (as the third way allows), then, in Hume's words, "it seems absurd to inquire for a general cause or first author." [63] The causal relation between any two beings A and B requires a temporal priority of the cause (A) over the effect (B). But if the effect exists eternally, it is senseless to speak of the eternal series having a first cause. But if God is not the first of an ordered series, but is that upon which the series as a whole depends, regardless of the number or temporal duration of its members, then, again in Hume's words, "Where then is the difficulty? But the *whole,* you say, wants a cause. . . . Did I show you the particular causes of each individual in a collection of twenty particles of matter, I should think it very unreasonable, should you afterwards ask me, what was the cause of the whole twenty." [64] Put otherwise, Flew continues, if the presence of each of five Eskimos on a streetcorner can be explained, there is no need for any further explanation of them as a group. Once the cause of each member of a series is known, no further causal questions are necessary. Whatever interpretation one cares to put on the "infinite series" sentence, then, a dead end is reached, either because none is possible or because nothing further is required. We have here "no launching pad of fact, and no force of argument, sufficient to project us outside the universe into the theologian's not-space beyond the stars." [65]

Before closing this discussion, there is one more aspect of the cosmological argument that bears brief review, that is, the logical status of the argument as a whole. At first glance there seems to be good reason for interpreting it as moving along hypothetico-deductive lines: an imperceptible entity (God) is postulated in order

---

[63] Hume, *Dialogues,* IX, p. 735.

[64] *Ibid.*

[65] Flew, *God,* p. 89. For Flew's own presentation of these objections see pp. 89–91.

to explain the existence of some fact or facts. There is, so far, no difficulty in this. An analogous procedure is found in many sciences in which puzzling facts, slips of the tongue, for example, are explained by means of an hypothesis which postulates the existence of a "transcendent" entity (an unconscious mind). Trouble lies, however, in the fact that in science a transcendent hypothesis is justified in terms of the consequences which may be deduced from it and which serve to verify or falsify it. But the conclusion of the cosmological argument has no deducible consequences that can verify or falsify it in the ordinary senses of those words. Hence, the argument seems cogent because of its similarity to unobjectionable hypothetico-deductive arguments which posit transcendent entities. But since it cannot be verified or falsified, it is not the kind of argument it pretends to be.[66]

Henry Veatch has suggested, however, that the cosmological argument is, properly interpreted, not meant to be analogous to this kind of argument at all. In the hypothetico-deductive method, the fact to be explained via an hypothesis is explained by being deducible from it as a necessary consequence. But the existence of a necessary being does not explain contingent beings in this way. Given, that is, the hypothesis of a necessary being in whom essence and existence are identical, it does not follow, at least in Aquinas' metaphysics, that there must be contingent beings. In the hypothetico-deductive method, the *explicans* does not logically imply the *explicandum*. In fact, one of the salient features of this method is that there is no logical method, either deductive or inductive, that allows us to get from the fact to be explained to the explanatory hypothesis. But in the cosmological argument, the movement is from the contingent to the necessary, the conditioned to the unconditioned, by virtue of the fact that the existence of the former *necessarily implies* the latter. "There is a necessary being"

---

[66] This is a summary of the argument in Herbert Feigl, "Critique of Intuition According to Scientific Empiricism," *Philosophy East and West,* VIII (1958), p. 12 (hereafter cited as Feigl, "Critique") as given by Veatch, "Knowledge-Claims," p. 392. An analogous criticism may be found in Flew, *God,* p. 71.

is not, then, an hypothesis formulated to account for the existence of the world of contingent beings, but is implied by the existence of that world.

What, then, is the logical character of the argument? It is, Veatch suggests, a straightforward, logically impeccable *modus ponens* argument of the form:

> If there are contingent beings, there is a necessary being.
> There are contingent beings.
> Therefore, there is a necessary being.[67]

But don't we now face the accusation (made, for example, by Ayer) that it is indefensible to infer the existence of an unobservable, transcendent, metaphysical entity from bases that are exclusively experiential? [68] If, Veatch counters, in science, when subject to falsification through a *modus tollens* form of argument, an hypothesis positing the existence of a transcendent entity is admissible, why should not a demonstration through *modus ponens* provide equal justification in metaphysics or theology? Veatch quotes Herbert Feigl as having written that "as long as one has a 'foothold' somewhere in direct experience, any sort of existent may well be accessible through knowledge by description. This, after all, is the only epistemological view which renders plausible our knowledge of unobserved and unobservable entities, as, e.g., in modern physics." [69] But this is just what the cosmological argument does. From a foothold in experience, it reaches knowledge by description of no less than a necessary being or God himself.[70]

Summary

In this chapter we have surveyed some of the ways in which analytic writers approach the traditional proofs for the existence of

---

[67] Veatch, "Knowledge-Claims," p. 404.

[68] Ayer, *Language*, p. 33.

[69] Feigl, "Critique," pp. 10–11, as given by Veatch, "Knowledge-Claims," p. 404.

[70] Veatch, "Knowledge-Claims," p. 404.

God. Many of the discussions bear witness to the philosophical seriousness with which this issue is now being entertained. We are far away from Ayer's casual dismissal of the whole question as metaphysical and therefore meaningless; we are, similarly, rapidly going beyond the catch phrases that were used in the past to dismiss any proof for the existence of God as a morass of linguistic and logical errors. Important discussions of proofs and the possibility of proofs for a transcendent being are current; dogmatic stands are being shed, other traditions and viewpoints are being heard, and writers are exhibiting a marked openness to previously excluded possibilities—even to the much-discredited ontological argument—signaling a growing interest in this deepest of metaphysical issues.

It is still too early to know where and how far all this is going. But we can register at least tentative disagreement with Henry Veatch's comment that anyone who enters serious discussion concerning the existence of God puts himself in danger of being taken for Anselm's fool.[71] It will probably be asking too much, however, to look to the analytic movement for a new proof for God's existence, as it seems more given to evaluating traditional proofs than to constructing new ones. This is due in part to the "positivist hangover" that still lingers on; despite the notable progress, there is still an undercurrent of uneasiness about metaphysics and metaphysical entities. But it is also due to the analytic method itself, which is perhaps most useful as a method of criticism rather than a method of discovery. Carefully constructed criticisms, however, could conceivably point the way to newer, and more acceptable, versions of older arguments, and a creative contribution may thereby be made in this important area.

---

[71] *Ibid.,* p. 391.

VII

Summary

We have come to a tentative end of our study. Tentative, because the analytic movement, born in the twentieth century, continues to develop and change and to shape much of the century's
philosophical thinking. Final verdicts concerning its place within
the *philosophia perennis* must wait until such a time as it may
have run its course. But seeking only tentative answers, what can
we say about the place of analysis in philosophy, and specifically
in the philosophy of religion? What has it shown us that we did
not know, or did not know as well, before?

Analysis arose after a philosophical period in which language,
precise expression, and the truths of common sense were accorded
minimal philosophical values. The proto-analysts Moore and Russell pleaded, on the one hand, for philosophical respect for what
everyone knew to be true and on the other, that certain philosophical problems arose from mistakes in "philosophical grammar."
Moore and Russell, however, still held to the view that a very important part of philosophy was the elaboration of an account of
reality as a whole.

But a more radical approach to philosophy was in the offing.
The Vienna Circle of Logical Positivism set out on a campaign of
reformation. This was premised on two related theses. First, that
it was not philosophy's task to give an account of reality or to
provide man with new facts about his world. This was the province of the positive sciences alone. Second, that philosophy's self-
purification was to be accomplished through the use of the verification principle which, allegedly based on certain general
considerations of language, would exclude from philosophy all
meaningless statements. Henceforth, philosophers would deal with

158

language and meaning alone; guided by the verification principle, they would take the fact-free statements of philosophy and exclude from them whatever was without meaning. The Vienna Circle confidently expected that a new and fruitful era of philosophizing was about to emerge.

Large portions of what was traditionally considered ethics, aesthetics, epistemology, and metaphysics were thus discarded; religion, too, since it traded in metaphysical entities, was ignored. Not only were philosophers forbidden to attend to metaphysical and religious accounts of reality; the ban went further: any such account was without cognitive content. Rejoicing in their freedom from the rubble of an unenlightened past, positivists could turn to proper philosophical pursuits—the analysis of ordinary language and, particularly, the language of positive science and mathematics.

But internal difficulties nagged at some key positivist conceptions, and many thinkers were led to believe that the verification principle, the chief weapon in the positivist arsenal, was itself defective. Serious doubts were expressed, too, concerning the philosopher's right to legislate concerning what man could and could not say, concerning the positivist theory of language and its erection of the language of science as paradigmatic for language in general, and concerning positivism's univocal conception of meaning and truth.

In his *Philosophical Investigations,* Ludwig Wittgenstein countered positivism on these issues. Language, he argued, did not have a single function, but a variety of functions, no one of which was the standard for all the rest. Men employ a variety of "language-games," each with its own rules, moves, "pieces," and aims. As for meaning and truth, as there are many different languages, so there are many different *meanings* and *truths*. In this new way of looking at things, philosophical problems were not caused by meaninglessness, but by the muddle that could arise from the workings of ordinary language and the failure to draw necessary distinctions among our many language-games. Analysis was the method by which philosophical disputes, all linguistically-generated according to Wittgenstein, could be dissipated. While positivists looked mainly to the language of science and mathematics for their subject matter, Wittgenstein and his followers looked to ordinary language.

How did religion fare in all of this? Since fundamental differences had begun to divide the analytic movement, two general ways of looking at religion emerged. Positivism had judged religious language to be emotive. But as that category turned out to include all nonsignificant but useful areas of language, it became so broad as to say nothing at all. What precise place do religious statements have in men's lives? And how are they connected with other statements men use? Positivist-leaning writers turned to these questions and tried to show that religious statements were only disguised ethical or ideological assertions, for example, or were nothing but statements of feelings or attitudes. Behind all this lay the idea that all religious statements were of a single type and could therefore be subsumed under one heading. Of course, whatever the heading might turn out to be, it was taken for granted that religious statements were deficient in cognitive value.

But the followers of Wittgenstein tended to see matters differently. Wittgenstein himself had found the language of religion troublesome, complicated, and sometimes muddled. But his judgments were based on piecemeal explorations and exemplified his desire to illuminate rather than exclude, to see what was happening rather than say what could or could not happen. His disciples followed in his spirit, and a number of limited studies were undertaken, often of one religious statement used in a particular way. For religious language in general, so the assumption goes, could not be characterized until one had seen what religious language in particular was all about. Various functions for religious discourse were thus identified. Religious statements could be used, for example, as invitations, definitions, accusations, and prescriptions. Behind some of these functions, some writers identified man's discernment of something that went beyond the "bare facts," and Christian religious language was seen to be tied to the believer's commitment to the person of Christ. Religious statements were held to be meaningful and also truth-functional in their own ways, which were not necessarily the ways in which other kinds of statements might be meaningful. Religious statements, it has been pointed out, are not "uniformly flat"; important ones use authorized models and live the life of a thousand qualifications in order to tell the believer something about God, while insuring that the God thus spoken of remains ineffable.

There are many ways of dealing with religious language other than the ones analysts have adopted. We have discussed three of the more prominent of these—ways that have had only a limited influence on analytic thinking. Those who connect religious language with religious experience have so far failed to present a fully viable alternative to positivism's contention that religious language is deficient in objective communication-value. The Thomistic doctrine of analogy, as well as the work of Tillich and existentialist theology in general, are far less influential than some might wish, because many analysts want no part either of metaphysics or of the metaphysical systems which support these positions. Old resolves and the attitudes they engender do not die easily. For perhaps the large majority of analysts, metaphysics of any kind is either hostile or unknown territory.

But some analysts have recently started to rediscover metaphysics and have suggested that even if it is not desirable to do metaphysics in the older neo-Hegelian way, it is perhaps possible to construct a metaphysics of some sort, descriptive metaphysics, for example. In this enterprise, the methods of analysis have been found useful—shades of Moore and Russell! For the philosophy of religion, this development has had at least one important consequence. The question of God's existence has always been in the background of discussions of the meaningfulness of religious statements, and the "return to metaphysics," if we may call it that, has led some to take a fresh look at this question, and by extension, at a host of other metaphysical topics connected with it. A great deal still remains to be done, not only in this area but in other areas of the philosophy of religion which have so far been forbidden ground: on the notion of miracles, the problem of evil, the question of immortality, and the language of theology (rather than religion) in general. If analysis can be fully purified of positivism's influence, it may prove to be an increasingly useful tool in problems of religion.

What, then, has analysis contributed to the perennial philosophy? While some may still hold that the wise man is not concerned with words, analysis has taught us that, indeed, wise men *must* be concerned with words, although it has also shown, through its limitations, that it is not enough to be concerned solely with words. Plato's *Sophist* eloquently argued that philosophy can exist only when the door is left open to communication; and Aristotle has warned us that intelligent communication requires that the meanings of terms be clearly understood by all. We have learned well what Bacon said too: words can become the idols of the mind, and the wise man, to be wise, must seek to eradicate those idols. Philosophers have long recognized that problems of language belong, in some sense, to them. Analysis has underscored this. But it has also shown that some philosophical problems (some would, of course, say *all*) have arisen because wise men have not been as concerned with language as they should have been, and that an analysis of the linguistic muddles that have given rise to these problems will also dissipate them. Analysis has brought to the forefront the area of philosophical linguistics has sketched some alternative descriptions of language, and has shown again that which Aristotle knew, that there is an intimate relationship between language and philosophy.

For many who are not themselves analysts, the methods and techniques which this movement has developed have already proved useful in clarifying issues and in sorting out the many strands that are so frequently involved in what might appear to be a simple philosophical puzzle. To know precisely what it is that one is handling is of enormous help in doing philosophy; to be able to see that a given problem may involve significant linguistic issues can save the wasted effort of trying to solve a problem at one level when the trouble really lies at another.

In dealing with problems in the philosophy of religion, analysis has helped dissipate simplistic approaches to religious language that might lead some to consider that all such language is of the same type—a confusion that can easily lead to further problems in religion proper. It has drawn attention to some of the different kinds of statements that make up religious discourse and has begun the long task of charting their similarities and differences. It has shown that religious language is problematical, largely because of its complexity. It has shown that religious meaning and truth is not the same as other kinds of meanings and truths with which men are familiar, and has indicated (sometimes in spite of itself) some of the mistakes that can be made if this fact is not recognized. In all of this, it can be of service to the ordinary man of faith no less than to the theologian by allowing him to gain a deeper understanding of the language he uses in expressing his faith.

Many look to philosophy for new insights into reality and to the philosophy of religion for what it can tell us about religious belief and practice. Here, analytic contributions are minimal. Analysis has been primarily a method of criticism rather than one that allows the discovery of new "facts"; it aims primarily at providing effective means whereby what others say can be critically evaluated and better understood. Philosophy, for analysts, is a discipline that does not tell us about the real, but tells us instead about those disciplines that deal with reality. Analysis can clarify and illuminate; and these are contributions of no small worth.

Bibliography

The following works were consulted in the preparation of this book. Those asterisked (∗) have been cited in the text.

Alston, William P. "Are Positivists Metaphysicians?" *The Philosophical Review*, LXIII (1954), 43–57.

————. "The Ontological Argument Revisited," *The Philosophical Review*, LXIX (1960), 452–474.(∗)

Ammerman, Robert R., ed. *Classics of Analytic Philosophy*. New York: McGraw-Hill, Inc., 1965.(∗)

Anderson, James F. *Natural Theology*. Milwaukee, Wis.: The Bruce Publishing Company, 1962.(∗)

————. *The Bond of Being*. St. Louis: Herder Book Co., 1949.(∗)

Anscombe, G. E. M. *An Introduction to Wittgenstein's Tractatus*. London: Hutchinson University Library, 1959.

————, and Geatch, P. T. *Three Philosophers: Aristotle, Aquinas, and Frege*. Oxford: Basil Blackwell, 1963.(∗)

Aquinas, Saint Thomas. *On the Truth of the Catholic Faith (Summa Contra Gentiles)*. 5 vols. Translated by Anton C. Pegis et al. Garden City, N.Y.: Image Books, 1955.(∗)

————. *D. Thomae Aquinatis Opera Omnia*. Edited by S. Frette and P. Mare. 32 vols. Paris: L. Vivès, 1871–1880.(∗)

————. *Summa Theologiae*. Translated by the Fathers of the English Dominican Province. 3 vols. New York: Benziger, 1947.(∗)

Aristotle. *The Basic Works*. Edited by Richard McKeon. New York: Random House, 1941.(∗)

Ashe, Geoffrey. "Meaning and Analogy," *The Hibbert Journal*, XLIX (1950–1951), 388–393.

Augustine, Saint. *Christian Instruction (De doctrina christiana)*. Translated by John J. Gavigan. *The Fathers of the Church*, vol. 2. New York: Fathers of the Church, Inc., 1947.(∗)

Ayer, A. J. *Language, Truth and Logic*. 2d ed. New York: Dover Publications Inc., n.d.(∗)

————. *The Foundations of Empirical Knowledge*. London: Macmillan and Co. Ltd., 1964.

————. *The Problem of Knowledge.* London: Macmillan and Co. Ltd., 1958.

————, ed. *Logical Positivism.* New York: The Free Press, 1959.

————, et al. *The Revolution in Philosophy.* London: Macmillan and Co. Ltd., 1960.

Baillie, D. M. *God Was In Christ.* London: Faber and Faber, Ltd., 1948.(*)

Baillie, John. *Our Knowledge of God.* New York: Charles Scribner's Sons, 1939.(*)

Baylis, C. A. "Facts, Propositions, Exemplification and Truth," *Mind,* LVII (1948), 459–479.

Bendall, Kent, and Ferré, Frederick. *Exploring the Logic of Faith.* New York: Association Press, 1962.

Berenda, Carlton W. "A Five-Fold Scepticism in Logical Empiricism," *Philosophy of Science,* XVII (1950), 123–132.

————. "On Verifiability, Simplicity, and Equivalence," *Philosophy of Science,* XIX (1952), 70–76.

Berthold, Frederick. "Logical Empiricism and Philosophical Theology," *The Journal of Religion,* XXXV (1955), 207–217.(*)

Binkley, Luther. "What Characterizes Religious Language?" *Journal for the Scientific Study of Religion,* II (1962), 18–22.(*)

Black, Max. *A Companion to Wittgenstein's* Tractatus. Ithaca, N.Y.: Cornell University Press, 1964.

————. "Some Questions About Emotive Meaning," *The Philosophical Review,* LVII (1948), 111–126.

Blackstone, William T. *The Problem of Religious Knowledge.* Englewood Cliffs, N.J.: Prentice-Hall, Inc., 1963.(*)

Bradley, Francis H. *Appearance and Reality.* 2d ed. New York: The Macmillan Co., 1902.(*)

————. *Ethical Studies.* 2d ed. Oxford: At the Clarendon Press, 1927.

Braithwaite, Richard B. *An Empiricist's View of the Nature of Religious Belief.* Cambridge: Cambridge University Press, 1955.(*)

Bunge, Mario. "Kinds and Criteria of Scientific Laws," *Philosophy of Science,* XXVIII (1961), 260–281.

Burbidge, John W. "The Language of Christian Faith," *Canadian Journal of Theology,* XII (1966), 21–26.

Burrill, Donald R., ed. *The Cosmological Arguments.* Garden City, N.Y.: Anchor Books, 1967.

Burtt, E. A., ed. *The English Philosophers from Bacon to Mill.* New York: The Modern Library, 1939.(*)

————. "What is Metaphysics?" *The Philosophical Review,* LIV (1945), 533–557.

Butchvarov, P. "Meaning-as-use and Meaning-as-correspondence," *Philosphy*, XXXV (1960), 314–325.

Camus, Albert. *The Myth of Sisyphus*. New York: Vintage Books, 1959.(*)

Carnap, Rudolf. *Introduction to Semantics* and *Formalization of Logic*. Cambridge, Mass.: Harvard University Press, 1959.(*)

————. *Le problème de la logique de la science*. Paris: Hermann et Cie., 1935.

————. *Meaning and Necessity*. Chicago: University of Chicago Press, 1947.

————. *Philosophy and Logical Syntax*. London: Kegan Paul, Trench, Trubner and Co. Ltd., 1935.(*)

————. "Testability and Meaning," *Philosophy of Science*, III, IV (1936, 1937), 420–471, 2–40.

————. *The Unity of Science*. Translated by M. Black. London: Kegan Paul, Trench, Trubner and Co. Ltd., 1934.(*)

Cartwright, Richard L. "Ontology and the Theory of Meaning," *Philosophy of Science*, XXI (1954), 316–325.

Castell, Aubrey. "Meanings: Emotive, Descriptive, and Critical," *Ethics*, LX (1949), 55–61.

Chapman, Raymond. "Language and Religious Experience," *Church Quarterly Review*, CLXII (1961), 323–330.

Charlesworth, Maxwell J. "Linguistic Analysis and Language About God," *International Philosophical Quarterly*, I (1961), 139–167.(*)

Chisholm, Roderick M. "Philosophers and Ordinary Language," *The Philosophical Review*, LX (1951), 317–328.

Church, Alonzo. "Review of Ayer's *Language, Truth and Logic*," *Journal of Symbolic Logic*, XIV (1949), 52–53.(*)

Coates, J. B. "God and the Positivists," *The Hibbert Journal*, L (1951–1952), 225–231.

Coburn, Robert C. "A Neglected Use of Theological Language," *Mind*, LXXII (1963), 369–385.(*)

————. "The Concept of God," *Religious Studies*, II (1966), 61–74.

Collins, James. "Analytic Theism and Demonstrative Inference," *International Philosophical Quarterly*, I (1961), 235–263.

————. "God as a Function in Modern Systems of Philosophy," *Proceedings of the American Catholic Philosophical Association*, XXVIII (1954), 1–17.

Copleston, Frederick. "A Note on Verification," *Mind*, LIX (1950), 522–529.

————. *Contemporary Philosophy*. Westminster, Md.: Newman Press, 1956.

————. "Some Reflections on Logical Positivism," *Dublin Review,* CCXXIV (1950), 71–86.

————. "The Oxford Analysts: The Revolution in Philosophy," *The Tablet,* CCVII, June 23, 1956, 587–589.

Corbishley, Thomas. "Do the Mystics Know?" *The Hibbert Journal,* L (1951–1952), 1–9.

Coval, S. "Worship, Superlatives, and Concept Confusion," *Mind,* LXVIII (1959), 218–222.

Cronbach, Abraham. "The Linguistics of Theism," *The Hibbert Journal,* LII (1953–1954), 9–16.(*)

Daitz, Edna. "The Picture Theory of Meaning," *Mind,* LXII (1953), 184–201.

Daly, C. B. "Logical Positivism, Metaphysics, and Ethics," *Irish Theological Quarterly,* XXIII (1956), 111–150.

Descartes, René. *The Philosophical Works of Descartes.* 2 vols. Translated by E. S. Haldane and G. R. T. Ross. New York: Dover Publications Inc., 1955.(*)

Dickie, Edgar P. *God is Light.* London: Hodder and Stoughton, 1953.(*)

Dilley, Frank B. "Is There Knowledge of God?" *The Journal of Religion,* XXXVIII (1958), 116–126.

Ducasse, Curt J. *A Philosophical Scrutiny of Religion.* London: Nisbet and Co., 1954.

————. "Christianity, Rationality, and Faith," *The Review of Religion,* XXII (1958), 121–136.(*)

Emmet, Dorothy M. *The Nature of Metaphysical Thinking.* London: Macmillan and Co. Ltd., 1945.

————. " 'Reason' in Recent Theological Discussion," *The Political Quarterly,* XXVI (1955), 276–285.

Erikson, Ralph W. "Metaphysics of a Logical Empiricist," *Philosophy of Science,* VII (1941), 320–328.

Esser, Gerard. "Metaphysics is Concerned with Tautology or Nonsense Statements," *Proceedings of the American Catholic Philosophical Association,* XXIX (1955), 176–195.

Evans, J. L. "On Meaning and Verification," *Mind,* LXII (1953), 1–19.

Ewing, Alfred C. "Meaninglessness," *Mind,* XLVI (1937), 347–364.

————. "Religious Assertions in the Light of Contemporary Philosophy," *Philosophy,* XXXII (1957), 206–218.(*)

Farmer, H. H. *Revelation and Religion.* London: Nisbet and Co., 1954.(*)

————. *Towards Belief in God.* New York: The Macmillan Co., 1943.(*)

Farrer, Austin. *Finite and Infinite*. Westminster: Dacre Press, 1943.(*)

―――. *The Glass of Vision*. Westminster: Dacre Press, 1948.

Feigl, Herbert. "Critique of Intuition According to Scientific Empiricism," *Philosophy East and West*, VIII (1958), 1–16.(*)

―――, and Sellars, W., eds. *Readings in Philosophical Analysis*. New York: Appleton-Century-Crofts, Inc., 1949.(*)

Ferré, Frederick. "Is Language About God Fraudulent?" *Scottish Journal of Theology*, XII (1959), 337–360.(*)

―――. *Language, Logic and God*. New York: Harper and Row, 1961.(*)

Ferré, N. F. S. *Reason in Religion*. London: Thomas Nelson, Ltd., 1963.

Feyerabend, Paul K., and Maxwell, Grover, eds. *Mind, Matter, and Method*. Minneapolis, Minn.: University of Minnesota Press, 1966.(*)

Flew, Antony. *God and Philosophy*. New York: Harcourt, Brace and World, Inc., 1966.(*)

―――. *Hume's Philosophy of Belief*. New York: Humanities Press, 1961.

―――, ed. *Logic and Language*. First and Second Series. New York: Doubleday Anchor, 1965.(*)

―――, and MacIntyre, Alasdair, eds. *New Essays in Philosophical Theology*. London: SCM Press, 1955.(*)

Foster, Michael. "Contemporary British Philosophy and Christian Belief," *Cross-Currents*, X (1960), 375–385.

Gibson, Alexander. "Empirical Evidence and Christian Faith," *The Journal of Religion*, XXXVI (1956), 24–35.(*)

Gill, Jerry H. "Wittgenstein and Religious Language," *Theology Today*, XXI (1964), 59–72.(*)

Glasgow, W. D. "Knowledge of God," *Philosophy*, XXXII (1957), 229–240.

Gomperz, Heindrich. "The Meaning of 'Meaning'," *Philosophy of Science*, VIII (1941), 157–183.

Gorovitz, Samuel, and Williams, Ron G. *Philosophical Analysis: An Introduction to Its Language and Techniques*. New York: Random House, 1965.(*)

Grice, H. P. "Meaning," *The Philosophical Review*, LXVI (1957), 377–388.

Griesbach, Marc F. "The Analysts and the Nature of Philosophy," *Proceedings of the American Catholic Philosophical Association*, XXXIV (1960), 210–215.

Hall, Thor. "An Analysis of *Simul Iustus et Peccator*," *Theology Today*, XX (1963), 174–182.

Hall, W. Arnold. "Religious Experience as a Court of Appeal," *The Hibbert Journal*, LIII (1954–1955), 365–371.

Hamilton, Kenneth. *The System and the Gospel.* New York: The Macmillan Company, 1963.(*)

Harris, Errol B. "The Status of Ethics," *Ethics,* LIX (1949), 172–180.

Hartshorne, Charles. "The Theistic Proofs," *Union Seminary Quarterly Review,* XX (1965), 115–129.

——— et al. "Further Fascination of the Ontological Argument," *Union Seminary Quarterly Review,* XVIII (1963), 243–255.

Hawkins, D. J. B. "Inquest on Logical Positivism," *The Month,* V (1951), 199–206.

———. *The Essentials of Theism.* New York: Sheed and Ward, 1950.(*)

———. "What Do the Proofs for the Existence of God Purport to Do?" *The Clergy Review,* XXXVII (1952), 321–332.

Hayner, Paul. "Analogical Predication," *The Journal of Philosophy,* LV (1958), 855–862.(*)

Henle, Paul. "Uses of the Ontological Argument," *The Philosophical Review,* LXX (1961), 102–109.(*)

Hempel, Carl G. "Problems and Changes in the Empiricist Criterion of Meaning," *Révue internationale de philosophie,* IV (1950), 41–62.(*)

Hepburn, Ronald. *Christianity and Paradox.* London: Watts, 1958.(*)

Hick, John. *Faith and Knowledge.* Ithaca, N.Y.: Cornell University Press, 1957.(*)

———. "Necessary Being," *Scottish Journal of Theology,* XIV (1961), 353–369.

———. "Theology and Verification," *Theology Today,* XVII (1960), 12–31.

Hinton, J. M. "Review of Tillich's *Theology of Culture,*" *Mind,* LXIX (1960), 424–426.(*)

Hook, Sidney, ed. *Religious Experience and Truth.* New York: New York University Press, 1961.(*)

Hospers, J. *An Introduction to Philosophical Analysis.* Englewood Cliffs, N.J.: Prentice-Hall, 1953.(*)

Inge, W. R. *Mysticism in Religion.* London: Hutchinson's University Library, n.d.(*)

Jay, C. Douglas. "Logical Analysis, Theological Positivism, and Metaphysics," *Canadian Journal of Theology,* IV (1958), 171–178.

Joad, Cyril E. M. "Logical Positivism and Theory of Knowledge," *The Hibbert Journal,* XLVIII (1949–1950), 57–65.

Kant, Immanuel. *Critique of Pure Reason.* Translated by N. K. Smith. London: Macmillan and Co. Ltd., 1958.(*)

Kaufman, Gordon. "Philosophy of Religion: Subjective or Objective?" *The Journal of Philosophy,* LV (1958), 57–70.(*)

Kelley, Alden D. "Can We Talk About God?" *Church Quarterly Review*, CLXIII (1962), 305–317.

Kelsey, David. *The Fabric of Paul Tillich's Theology*. New Haven, Conn.: Yale University Press, 1967.(*)

Kennick, William E. "The Language of Religion," *The Philosophical Review*, LXV (1956), 56–71.(*)

Klubertanz, George. *St. Thomas Aquinas on Analogy*. Chicago: Loyola University Press, 1960.

Korner, Stephen. "The Meaning of Some Metaphysical Propositions," *Mind*, LVII (1948), 275–293.

Kraft, Victor. *The Vienna Circle*. Translated by A. Pap. New York: Philosophical Library, 1953.(*)

Laing, B. M. "Hume's *Dialogues Concerning Natural Religion*," *Philosophy*, XII (1937), 175–190.

Lazerowitz, Morris. "Are Self-Contradictory Expressions Meaningless?" *The Philosophical Review*, LVIII (1949), 563–584.

———. "Strong and Weak Verification," *Mind*, XLVIII (1939), 202–213.

———. "Strong and Weak Verification, II," *Mind*, LIX (1950), 345–357.

———. "The Positivistic Use of 'Nonsense'," *Mind*, LV (1964), 247–255.

Leibniz, G. W. *Leibniz: Philosophical Writings*. Translated by Mary Morris. London: J. M. Dent and Sons, Ltd., 1934.(*)

Leon, Philip. "The Meaning of Religious Propositions," *The Hibbert Journal*, LIII (1954–1955), 151–156.

Lewis, H. D., ed. *Contemporary British Philosophy, 3rd Series*. 2d ed. London: George Allen and Unwin, 1961.

Lewy, Casimir. "Entailment and Empirical Propositions," *Mind*, LV (1946), 74–78.

Lloyd, A. C. "Empiricism, Sense Data, and Scientific Languages," *Mind*, LIX (1950), 57–70.

Lunn, Arnold. "Miracles—the Scientific Approach," *The Hibbert Journal*, XLVIII (1949–1950), 240–246.

MacIntyre, Alasdair, ed. *Metaphysical Beliefs*. London: SCM Press, 1957.

MacIntyre, John. "Analogy," *Scottish Journal of Theology*, XXII (1959), 1–20.(*)

Macquarrie, John. "How Can We Think of God?" *Theology Today*, XX (1965), 194–204.

———. *Twentieth-Century Religious Thought*. New York: Harper and Row, 1963.(*)

Malcolm, Norman. "Anselm's Ontological Argument," *The Philosophical Review*, LXIX (1960), 41–62.(*)

————. *Ludwig Wittgenstein, A Memoir*. London: Oxford University Press, 1958.

Margolis, Joseph. "What is Religious Truth?" *The Review of Religion*, XX (1955), 38–46.

Martin, C. B. *Religious Belief*. Ithaca, N.Y.: Cornell University Press, 1959.

Mascall, Eric L. *Existence and Analogy*. London: Longmans, Green and Co., 1949.(*)

————. "The Doctrine of Analogy," *Cross Currents*, I (1951), 38–57.

Masterman, Margaret. "Linguistic Philosophy and Dogmatic Theology," *Theology*, LIV (1951), 82–89.

Matthews, Gareth. "Theology and Natural Theology," *The Journal of Philosophy*, LXI (1964), 99–108.(*)

Mavrodes, George I. "God and Verification," *Canadian Journal of Theology*, X (1964), 187–191.(*)

McInerny, Ralph. *The Logic of Analogy*. The Hague: Nijhoff, 1961.(*)

McKelway, A. J. *The Systematic Theology of Paul Tillich*. Richmond, Va.: John Knox Press, 1964.(*)

McKinnon, Alastair. "The Meaning of Religious Assertions," *Encounter*, XXI (1960), 398–407.(*)

————. "Unfalsifiability and Religious Belief," *Canadian Journal of Theology*, XII (1966), 118–125.(*)

McMullin, Ernan. "The Analytic Approach to Philosophy," *Proceedings of the American Catholic Philosophical Association*, XXXIV (1960), 50–79.

McPherson, Thomas H. "The Existence of God," *Mind*, LIX (1950), 545–550.

Migne, *Patrologia Latina*. 221 vols. Paris: Apud Garnier Fratres, 1844–.(*)

Miles, T. R. "On Excluding the Supernatural," *Religious Studies*, I (1965), 141–150.(*)

————. *Religion and the Scientific Outlook*. New York: Humanities Press, 1959.(*)

Miller, David L. "Meaning and Verification," *The Philosophical Review*, LII (1943), 604–609.

Miller, Robert G. "Linguistic Analysis and Metaphysics," *Proceedings of the American Catholic Philosophical Association*, XXXIV (1960), 80–109.

Mitchell, Basil, ed. *Faith and Logic*. London: George Allen and Unwin, Ltd., 1957.(*)

Moore, G. E. *Ethics*. London: Oxford University Press, 1963.

————. *Philosophical Papers*. New York: Collier Books, 1959.

————. *Philosophical Studies*. Paterson, N.J.: Littlefield, Adams and Co., 1959.

————. *Principia Ethica*. Cambridge: At the University Press, 1903.

————. *Some Main Problems of Philosophy*. London: Allen and Unwin, 1953.(*)

Nelson, Everett J. "The Verification Theory of Meaning," *The Journal of Religion*, XXIX (1951), 155–168.

Newman, James R. *The World of Mathematics*. 4 vols. New York: Simon and Schuster, 1956.(*)

Nielsen, Kai. "Eschatological Verification," *Canadian Journal of Theology*, IX (1963), 271–281.(*)

————. "God and Verification Again," *Canadian Journal of Theology*, XI (1965), 135–141.(*)

————. "On Fixing the Reference Range of 'God'," *Religious Studies*, II (1966), 13–36.(*)

————. "On Speaking of God," *Theoria*, XXVIII (1962), 110–137.(*)

————. "On Talk About God," *The Journal of Philosophy*, LV (1958), 888–890.(*)

O'Neill, Joseph E., ed. *The Encounter with God*. New York: The Macmillan Company, 1960.

Otto, Rudolf. *The Idea of the Holy*. New York: Oxford University Press, 1958.

Owens, Joseph. *An Interpretation of Existence*. Milwaukee, Wis.: The Bruce Publishing Co., 1968.(*)

Pap, Arthur. *Semantics and Necessary Truth*. New Haven, Conn.: Yale University Press, 1958.

————. "Types and Meaninglessness," *Mind*, LXIX (1960), 41–54.

Passmore, John. *A Hundred Years of Philosophy*. New York: Basic Books, 1957.(*)

Pears, D. F. "The Philosophy of Wittgenstein," *The New York Review of Books*, XII (Jan. 16, 1969), 21–30.

————, ed. *The Nature of Metaphysics*. London: Macmillan and Co. Ltd., 1957.

Pegis, Anton C., ed. *The Wisdom of Catholicism*. New York: Random House, 1949.(*)

————, transl. *On the Truth of the Catholic Faith*. 5 vols. Garden City, N.Y.: Image Books, n.d.

Phelan, Gerald B. *St. Thomas and Analogy*. Milwaukee, Wis.: Marquette University Press, 1941.(*)

"Philosophy and Beliefs; A Discussion Between Four Oxford Philosophers," *Twentieth Century*, CLVII (1955), 495–521.

Pitcher, George. *The Philosophy of Wittgenstein.* Englewood Cliffs, N.J.: Prentice-Hall, Inc., 1964.

————, ed. *Wittgenstein: The Philosophical Investigations.* Garden City, N.Y.: Anchor Books, 1966.

Plantinga, Alvin. "Analytic Philosophy and Christianity," *Christianity Today,* VIII, Oct. 25, 1963, 17–20.

————. *God and Other Minds.* Ithaca, N. Y.: Cornell University Press, 1967.(*)

————, ed. *The Ontological Argument.* New York: Doubleday Anchor Books, 1965.(*)

Plato, *Dialogues.* 2 vols. Translated by Benjamin Jowett. New York: Random House, 1937.(*)

Pole, David. *The Later Philosophy of Wittgenstein.* London: The Athlone Press, University of London, 1958.

Popper, Karl. *The Logic of Scientific Discovery.* London: Hutchinson and Co., 1959.(*)

Presley, C. F. "Laws and Theories in the Physical Sciences," *The Australasian Journal of Philosophy,* XXXII (1954), 79–103.

Pringle-Pattison, A. Seth. *Studies in the Philosophy of Religion.* Oxford: At the Clarendon Press, 1930.(*)

Prior, Arthur N. "Facts, Propositions and Entailment," *Mind,* LVII (1948), 62–68.

Ramsey, Ian T. *Models and Mystery.* London: Oxford University Press, 1964.(*)

————. *Religious Language: An Empirical Placing of Theological Phrases.* New York: The Macmillan Company, 1963.(*)

Reichenbach, Hans. *Experience and Prediction.* Chicago: The University of Chicago Press, 1938.(*)

Rickman, H. P. "Metaphysics as the Creation of Meaning," *The Hibbert Journal,* LII (1953–1954), 166–174.

Rose, Mary C. "The Language of Religion," *Anglican Theological Review,* XL (1958), 108–119.(*)

Ross, James F. "Analogy as a Rule of Meaning for Religious Language," *International Philosophical Quarterly,* I (1961), 468–502.

Russell, Bertrand. *An Inquiry into Meaning and Truth.* London: George Allen and Unwin, 1940.

————. *Human Knowledge, Its Scope and Limits.* New York: Simon and Schuster, 1948.

————. *Introduction to Mathematical Philosophy.* London: George Allen and Unwin, Ltd., 1919.(*)

————. *Logic and Knowledge.* London: George Allen and Unwin, Ltd., 1956.(*)

————. *My Philosophical Development*. New York: Simon and Schuster, 1959.

————. *Mysticism and Logic*. Garden City, N.Y.: Doubleday Anchor Books, 1957.

————. *The Analysis of Mind*. London: George Allen and Unwin, Ltd., 1921.(*)

Ryan, Columba. "Metaphysics and Language; An Introduction to the Problem," *Blackfriars*, XXXII (1951), 462–468.

Schlesinger, G. *Method in the Physical Sciences*. London: Routledge and Kegan Paul, Ltd., 1963.(*)

Schlick, Moritz. "Die Kausalität in der gegenwärtigen Physik," *Die Naturwissenschaften*, XIX (1931), 145–162.(*)

————. *Problems of Ethics*. Translated by D. Rynin. New York: Prentice-Hall, Inc., 1939.(*)

Schmidt, Paul F. "Is there Religious Knowledge?" *The Journal of Philosophy*, LV (1958), 529–538.

Schopenhauer, Arthur. *The Fourfold Root of the Principle of Sufficient Reason*. Translated by Mme. Karl Hillebrand. Rev. ed. London: George Bell and Sons, 1897.(*)

Sellars, Roy W. "A Correspondence Theory of Truth," *The Journal of Philosophy*, XXXVIII (1941), 645–654.

Shideler, Emerson W. "Logical Treatment of Religious Propositions," *Journal of Bible and Religion*, XXIII (1955), 278–285.

Smart, Ninian. "Interpretation and Mystical Experience," *Religious Studies*, I (1965), 75–87.

Smith, Henry B. "What is Religious Knowledge?" *The Hibbert Journal*, XLIV (1945–1946), 54–58.

Smith, Robert V. "Analytic Philosophy and Religious/Theological Language," *Journal of Bible and Religion*, XXX (1962), 101–108.

Smith, T. V., ed. *Philosophers Speak for Themselves*. 4 vols. Chicago: University of Chicago Press, 1956.(*)

Spiegelberg, Herbert. "Supernaturalism or Naturalism: A Study in Meaning and Verifiability," *Philosophy of Science*, XVIII (1951), 339–368.

Stace, W. T. "Some Misinterpretations of Empiricism," *Mind*, LXVII (1958), 465–484.

Stark, Rodney. "A Taxonomy of Religious Experience," *Journal for the Scientific Study of Religion*, V (1965), 97–116.

Steinus, Erik. *Wittgenstein's Tractatus; A Critical Exposition of its Main Lines of Thought*. Ithaca, N.Y.: Cornell University Press, 1960.

Stevenson, Charles L. "Meaning: Descriptive and Emotive," *The Philosophical Review*, LVII (1948), 127–144.

"Symposium: Are Religious Dogmas Cognitive and Meaningful?" *The Journal of Philosophy,* LI (1954), 145–172.

"Symposium on Emotive Meaning," *The Philosophical Review,*" LVII (1948), 111–157.

"Symposium: The Concept of God," *The Journal of Philosophy,* LVII (1960), 689–734.

"Symposium: The Nature of Analysis," *The Journal of Philosophy,* LIV (1957), 741–766.

"Symposium: The Present Status of Natural Theology," *The Journal of Philosophy,* LV (1958), 925–944.(*)

Tavard, George. *Paul Tillich and the Christian Message.* New York: Charles Scribner's Sons, 1961.(*)

———. "Tillich: Christ as the Answer to Existential Anguish," *Continuum,* IV (1966), 3–12.

The New Testament in Modern English. Translated by J. B. Phillips. London: Geoffrey Bles, 1960.(*)

The Poems of St. John of the Cross. Translated by John F. Nims. New York: Grove Press, Inc., 1959.

Tillich, Paul. *Biblical Religion and the Search for Ultimate Reality.* Chicago: University of Chicago Press, 1955.

———. *Dynamics of Faith.* New York: Harper and Brothers, 1957.

———. *My Search for Absolutes.* New York: Simon and Schuster, 1967.

———. *Systematic Theology.* 3 vols. Chicago: University of Chicago Press, 1951, 1957, 1963.(*)

———. *The Courage to Be.* New Haven: Yale University Press, 1952.

Torrance, Thomas. "The Scientific Character of Theological Statements," *Dialog,* IV (1965), 112–117.

Toulmin, Stephen. "Ludwig Wittgenstein," *Encounter,* XXXII (1969), 58–71.(*)

———. *The Philosophy of Science.* New York: Harper Torchbooks, 1960.

Trethowan, Dom Illyd. "In Defence of Theism—A Reply to Kai Nielsen," *Religious Studies,* II (1966), 37–48.(*)

Turner, Vincent. "Preliminaries to Theism," *The Dublin Review,* CCXXV (1951), 12–27.

Urmson, J. O. *Philosophical Analysis.* Oxford: Clarendon Press, 1966.(*)

Van Buren, Paul. "Christian Education *Post Mortem Dei*," *Religious Education,* LX (1965), 4–10.(*)

———. "The Dissolution of the Absolute," *Religion in Life,* XXXIV (1965), 334–342.(*)

176   BIBLIOGRAPHY

————. "Theology in the Context of Culture," *The Christian Century*, LXXXII, no. 14, April 7, 1965, 428–430.(*)
————. *The Secular Meaning of the Gospel.* New York: The Macmillan Company, 1963.(*)
Von Mises, R. *Positivism, a Study in Human Understanding.* Translated by J. Bernstein and R. G. Newton. Cambridge, Mass.: Harvard University Press, 1951.
Warnock, G. J. *English Philosophy Since 1900.* New York: Oxford University Press, 1966.(*)
Weiss, Paul. "Philosophy and Faith," *The Journal of Religion,* XXVI (1946), 278–282.
White, Alan R. *G. E. Moore; A Critical Exposition.* Oxford: Basil Blackwell, 1958.
Wieman, Henry N. "Can God be Perceived?" *The Journal of Religion,* XXIII (1943), 23–32.
Williams, Bernard, and Montefiore, Alan, eds. *British Analytic Philosophy.* London: Routledge and Kegan Paul, 1966.(*)
Williams, Daniel D. "Theology and Truth," *The Journal of Religion,* XXII (1942), 382–397.
Wilson, J. B. "Religious Assertions," *The Hibbert Journal,* LVI (1957–1958), 148–160.(*)
Wilson, John. *Philosophy and Religion.* London: Oxford University Press, 1961.(*)
Wisdom, John. "Metaphysics and Verification," *Mind,* XLVII (1938), 452–498.
————. "Positivism," *Mind,* LIV (1945), 65–70.
Wittgenstein, Ludwig. *Lectures and Conversations on Aesthetics, Psychology, and Religious Belief.* Edited by Cyril Barrett. Oxford: Basil Blackwell, 1966.(*)
————. *Notebooks, 1914–1916.* Edited by G. H von Wright and G. E. M. Anscombe. Oxford: Basil Blackwell, 1961.
————. *Philosophical Investigations.* Translated by G. E. M. Anscombe. New York: The Macmillan Company, 1953.(*)
————. *Tractatus Logico-Philosophicus.* Translated by D. F. Pears and B. F. McGuiness. London: Routledge and Kegan Paul, 1961.(*)
Woods, G. F. "The Use of Analogy in Christian Theology," *Journal of Theological Studies,* VII (1956), 226–238.
Zuurdeeg, Willem. "The Nature of Theological Language," *The Journal of Religion,* XL (1960), 1–8.(*)

Index

Abraham, 87
Aesthetic Judgments, and positivism, 25f.
Alston, William, P., 106 n.44; 107 n.45; 108 n.51; 110 n.55; 126; 128 n.10
—on the ontological argument, 128ff.
Analogy, 161
—and analytic philosophy, 101f.; and Thomas Aquinas, 92ff.; and authority, 100; criticisms, 95ff., 99ff.; and Frederick Ferré, 98; and Paul Hayner, 97f.; and religious language, 92ff.; purposes in religious language, 99ff.; types, 93ff.
Analysis (Analytic Philosophy)
—and analogy, 95ff.; definition, 4 n.4; and English philosophy, 8f.; and metaphysics, 16f., 42f.; and perennial philosophy, 162f.; and reason and revelation, 4f.; and Russell and Moore, 12f.; and Tillich's theology, 110f. *See also* English Philosophy; Vienna Circle of Logical Positivism; Wittgenstein.
Analytic Statements, 20f.
Anderson, James F., 92 n.1; 138 n.33
Anscombe, G. E. M., 153f.
Anselm, St., 136. *See also* Ontological Argument.

Aquinas, St. Thomas, 2; 65; 85; 99; 112; 152f.
—on analogy, 92ff.; cosmological argument, 150; criticism of ontological argument, 125, 140f. on infinite regress, 152ff.; on language and theology, 9; on necessary being, 138ff.; on reason and revelation, 2; on religious language, 61, 92ff.; on self-evident statements, 139ff.; teleological argument, 143ff.
Aristotle, 1; 9; 162
Augustine, St., 123; 125
Ayer, Alfred Jules, 10; 15f.; 156f.
—and death of metaphysics, 15; on ethics, metaphysics, and aesthetics, 25ff.; on religious language, 27ff.; on task of philosophy, 15f.; verification principle, 20ff.

Bacon, Francis, 20ff.
Baillie, D. M., 98 n.22
Baillie, John, 112 n.59
Being-Itself, 102ff.
—and God, 103; and religious symbols, 106ff. *See also* Tillich, Paul.
Berkeley, George,10
Berthold, Frederick, 112 n.59
Binkley, Luther, 69 n.6
Blackstone, William T., 96 n.14; 97 n.20; 111 n.57; 117 n.67

Philosophy of Science, and philosophy of religion, 6f.

Planck, Max, 14

Plantinga, Alvin, on cosmological argument, 150

Plato, 8f; 11; 63; 162

Popper, Karl, 25 n.29

Positivism. *See* Vienna Circle of Logical Positivism.

Pringle-Pattison, A. Seth, 6

Proposition, 20 n.20

Pseudo-Proposition, 20 n.20

Ramsey, Ian T., 82f.; 85 n.41

—on models, 73ff.; on religious language, 71ff.; on religious situations, 70f.

Ranier, A. C. A., 141

Reality, nature of, and positivism, 17f.

Reason and Revelation, 2

—and analytic philosophy, 3ff.; and Greek philosophy, 1; in medieval period, 2; in modern philosophy, 3; and nineteenth-century philosophers, 3f.

Reichenbach, Hans, 24 n.26

Relational Language, and God, 99f.

Religion and Philosophy. *See* Reason and Revelation.

Religious Belief

—Curt J. Ducasse on, 58; psychological importance, 58; reasons for, 88f.; its sources, 75f.; Wittgenstein on, 38f.

Religious Experience

—criticism of knowledge based on, 116ff.; and experience of color, 115, 117f.; objectivity of, 114ff.; and religious language, 112ff.

Religious Language

—Thomas Aquinas on, 61, 92ff.;

and attitudes, 60; A. J. Ayer on, 27 nn.31, 32, 33; 28f.; R. B. Braithwaite on, 53f.; and Christ, 77ff., 80, 83ff.; and commitment, 52, 70f.; I. M. Crombie on, 75ff.; Abraham Cronbach on, 59f.; its "essential" element, 62f.; as evaluative of experience, 59f.; and evil, 86ff.; and experience, 49f., 84ff.; and facts, 51f.; and falsification, 46, 49; Frederick Ferré on, 79ff.; Antony Flew on, 46; functions of, 67ff.; Richard M. Hare on, 47 n.11, 48; John Hick on, 50; as historical problem, 53; and hypotheses, 50f.; and ideological statements, 57f.; and incomprehensibility, 46f.; and the inexpressible, 60f.; as interpretive of experience, 50f.; Gordon Kaufman on, 58f.; William E. Kennick on, 60; John Macquarrie on, 81f.; Thomas McPherson on, 60f.; and metaphysical systems, 80f.; T. R. Miles, on, 54ff.; Basil Mitchell on, 48f.; and models, 73ff., 84ff.; and moral assertions, 53f.; and negative language, 72; and non-symbolic statements, 104; and object language, 71; and positive language, 72f.; psychological value, 58; Ian Ramsey on, 70ff.; and religious discernment, 70; and religious experience, 112ff.; as resolution of human problems, 58f; and subjective meanings, 58f.; and tautologies, 71f.; Paul Tillich on, 103ff.; and truth, 80ff.; and verification, 27ff.; Bernard Williams on, 46f.; Wittgenstein on, 38ff.;